THE DEEP STATE

THE DEEP STATE

A HISTORY OF SECRET AGENDAS AND SHADOW GOVERNMENTS

IAN FITZGERALD

I would like to thank the team at Arcturus, especially Vanessa
Daubney for giving me the opportunity to write this book and
John Turing for making sure that I did – with a welcome blend
of sound judgement, excellent advice and very much appreciated
patience. A big thank you also to Diana Vowles for copy editing
the manuscript and Dean Rockett for his proofreading endeavours.
They definitely helped to spare my blushes on more than one
occasion, and any mistakes, errors and omissions that remain
are all my own. I would also like to acknowledge the journalists,
reporters, writers and researchers around the world whose work
helped to inspire and inform this book.

CONTENTS

INTRODUCTION

'In all ages, whatever the form and name of government, be it monarchy, republic, or democracy, an oligarchy lurks behind the façade.'

Ronald Syme, *The Roman Revolution* (1939)

WHAT ARE GOVERNMENTS FOR? It's a big question, with many answers, depending on your viewpoint. At a very basic level, most people would agree that governments exist to protect their citizens from harm, to guarantee them a framework in which to live their lives safely and fairly. But not everyone sees it that way. For deep states, governments are merely the vehicles by which they advance their interests; citizens, by contrast, are merely pedestrians, bystanders to be knocked down if they get in the way.

For as long as there have been nation states, there have been deep states manipulating or undermining them. In this book we shall begin with Ancient Greece and Rome and end around the time of the election of Donald Trump as president of the United States and the UK's Brexit referendum of 2016, exploring how deep states manifest themselves in every age and in all circumstances. So ubiquitous are they that once you start looking, it's tempting to rethink civilization as one great unbroken chain of vested interests controlling events while kings, queens, emperors, popes, princes, politicians and presidents act as front-men and -women for history's true power-brokers. That may ultimately be something of an overstatement – but only just.

While deep states undoubtedly exist, they take a variety of forms. Aristocratic vested interests are the oldest examples we have, arising in the classical world as a reaction to then-novel experiments in government we today call democracy and republicanism. Military deep states came next, and, as we'll see, have never quite gone away, with a lineage running from the Praetorian Guard of the Roman world to the generals controlling Egypt, Pakistan, Thailand, Myanmar and elsewhere.

From there, the bad actors come thick and fast. As the institutions of government developed in the modern world, so did the institutional or bureaucratic deep state, a body concerned more with its own self-preservation than the interests of the state it nominally serves. Similarly, with the rise of trade, business, finance and commerce, so corporate deep states emerged to capitalize – literally and otherwise – on the enormous riches and power available, making and breaking governments and using their limitless resources to buy politicians, influence the judiciary and set a legislative agenda that favours profits over people. Organized crime has long understood that its needs and wants are also best served by cultivating political leaders, and few do it better than the mafia deep states of Italy and the USA and the ultra-violent and impoverishing narco-states of South America that destroy their civil societies as they amass vast fortunes.

Not all governments are acted upon, of course. Some are highly competent deep state operators themselves. China, for example, is building up a roster of client states across Africa, most notably in Zimbabwe, while Russia's hidden hand today extends as far as Syria's presidential palace and, it is suggested, to the White House in Washington D.C. and 10 Downing Street in London. More surprisingly, perhaps, the religious republic of Iran is fast becoming a deep state superpower across the Middle East, exporting its divisive version of Islam to an already troubled region with predictably bloody results. Then there are the shadow states that claim to act in their nations' interests but always prioritize their own agendas first and foremost, notably the government of Vladimir Putin in Russia and the 40-year reign of the Christian Democrats and the Socialists in Italy, practitioners of a form of state-sponsored kleptocracy that hides in plain sight and ruthlessly suppresses any form of dissent or opposition.

In addition, the past 20 years or so has seen a new form of deep state enter the fray. The rise of computing, mobile technology and the rapid growth of the internet as a means of communicating and sharing information has given birth to digital deep states whose size and reach has the potential to eclipse any form of undue influence that has ever gone before. At the same time, the cyberworld presents every existing deep state – corporate, political, bureaucratic, criminal, military – with new opportunities to extend their interests and influence ever further. It's a challenge they are surely up to. Adam Smith, the founding father of economics, wrote in *The Wealth of Nations* that 'People of the same trade seldom meet together, even for merriment and diversion, but the conversation ends in a conspiracy against the public.' It's an insight that's as true today as it was when Smith's book was published in 1776. Smith saw that a tendency towards deep state activity is an almost natural outcome of any interaction between power and money – and the bigger the interaction the deeper the state.

There are, sadly, hundreds of examples of deep-state activity to look at across the millennia. This book can only cover a fraction of them, so the focus here is on quality rather than quantity, taking in some of the most representative instances of deep-state subterfuge and largely favouring the modern era. It covers almost every continent, journeys back to the past and looks to the future, too – and what emerges clearly is that while the *where*, the *when* and the *who* of deep states may change, the *why* remains the same.

CHAPTER 1

HISTORICAL DEEP STATES

IT'S TEMPTING TO think of the deep state as a relatively modern phenomenon, but a look back through history reveals examples in every place and in every time. The deep state's aim has always been consistent, too: to further its own interests against those of the ruling authority.

In this chapter we'll look at how the various types of deep state have been established over the millennia. There's the oligarchic deep state of traditional elites, which arose in the very first democratic city-state, Ancient Athens, and then in republican Rome. Then there is the military deep state, embodied in the Praetorian Guard and in the legions of the Roman Empire, and later in the General Staff in Imperial Japan. The Ottoman

Empire of the 19th century best exemplifies an early example of the bureaucratic deep state, where concerned (and self-interested) civil servants and government officials work behind the scenes to control regimes whose activities they disagree with. Finally, we shall explore how ideological deep states in France and Germany acted in the aftermath of the Franco-Prussian War of 1870–71, and how their host states reacted in return.

THE OLIGARCHY OF ANCIENT ATHENS

In 508 BCE, the Athenian lawgiver Cleisthenes introduced a programme of political reform that he called *demokratia* ('rule by the people'). In 'inventing' democracy, Cleisthenes' aim had been to ameliorate rising tensions between the traditional oligarchic elites that had dominated Athenian politics since time immemorial and the growing 'middle class' of merchants and citizens who wanted a say in how the city-state was run. However, from its inception, democracy was susceptible to interference and manipulation by groups looking to prioritize their interests over the greater good. In Ancient Athens, this meant the formation of an oligarchic deep state to steal back the power that democracy had forced it to share with the lower orders.

The oligarchs fight back

While Cleisthenes and his successors made the new machinery of government as tamper-proof as possible, the oligarchs nevertheless found a way in. The Assembly is probably Athens' most famous example of the democratic process at work, a 'parliament' open to all of the city-state's 40,000 male citizens. But a more important organ of government from a deep-state point of view was the Boule. This was the office that did most of the day-to-day work of civic life. Crucially, it controlled the political agenda by deciding which legislation was put before the Assembly. Membership of the Boule was decided by the drawing of lots and this should have made it immune to corruption – but historical records show a higher than normal proportion of oligarchic citizens served on it, although how they managed to rig the lottery is not known.

Our rosy view of Athenian democracy certainly needs revisiting. As the classicist Claire Taylor has pointed out, 'Every level of Athenian politics was riddled with corruption, from the most important orators to the smallest deme election.' Between 6 and 10 per cent of senior public officials were tried on charges of bribery during Athens' golden age, with around half of them convicted. Much of this was fairly low-level corruption and favour-trading, but underlying it all was the constant chipping away by Athens' richest, most prominent and often competing families at the edifice of popular rule. There is even an argument to say that Cleisthenes introduced democracy partly to protect his own influential oligarchic family, the Alcmaeonidae, against a powerful rival clan, the Peisistratids. From 546 to 510 BCE, the Peisistratid family had ruled Athens as tyrants and had exiled Cleisthenes' Alcmaeonidae kin from the city. After helping to oust the Peisistratids in 510 BCE, Cleisthenes saw that continuing the cycle of rule by one family after another was unproductive and that a new approach to government was needed. In that sense, it could be said that while democracy grew out of good intentions the motivations behind it were self-interested as much as pragmatic. It's one of the great 'what ifs' of history to ponder whether democracy would even have been invented if the Peisistratids and the Alcmaeonidae had got on better.

This tension between democratic intent and oligarchic motivation mounted following the outbreak in 431 BCE of the Peloponnesian War, Athens' long-running conflict with its main regional rival, Sparta – an authoritarian, militaristic city-state much admired by those of an oligarchic cast of mind. As the war progressed, with periodic victories and defeats on both sides, Athens' oligarchic deep state began the process of undermining their home state's democracy once and for all. They were galvanized by works of propaganda, such as a widely circulated pamphlet called *The Athenian Constitution*. Its anonymous author was credited as the Old Oligarch, and the piece served as a rallying call for the 'best and most qualified' to impose their rule over 'the vulgar people'.

The end of an era

The war came to a head in 411 BCE, when Athens suffered a militarily devastating and financially catastrophic defeat by Sparta in Sicily. As a wave of popular unrest broke out in Athens, the oligarchs encouraged and funded attacks on public buildings and even on public officials. A group of aristocrats, led by the statesman Antiphon and the rogue Athenian general Alcibiades (an Alcmaeonidae, no less, who had been exiled from the city and had defected to Sparta), seized power and installed a government of prominent oligarchs known as the Four Hundred.

Within a year the coup had been overturned, but the damage to Athens' democracy had been done. The war with Sparta limped on for several more years, but when it finally ended in 404 BCE with Athens' total defeat a Spartan-imposed dictatorship of the Thirty Tyrants assumed control. Democracy was restored once more in 403 BCE, but was ended for good when Philip of Macedon conquered Greece in 338 BCE.

Fortunately, democracy did not disappear with the Athenian city-state. It survived and grew and evolved in Europe and then around the world, but so did the deep state virus that attached itself to the body politic and which remains to this day, dormant in many cases but very active in others.

REPUBLICAN AND IMPERIAL ROME

Ancient Roman history divides into two eras: the republic, which traditionally began in 509 BCE, and the empire, initiated by the rule of Augustus from 27 BCE. In deep-state terms, this translates to an oligarchic secret network interfering in the republican period, exemplified in the fate of the reforming Gracchi brothers, while for the Imperial epoch it is represented by the creeping influence of a military shadow government that ultimately tired of acting behind the scenes and took power for itself.

Defeating the Gracchi

Legend has it that Rome was founded in 753 BCE, on 21 April to be exact, by the brothers Romulus and Remus. It became a republic in 509 BCE when the last king was expelled from the city, and from that time onwards Romans were fiercely protective of their royalty-free government. But, as in Ancient Athens, the form of government Romans opted for was one dominated by the oligarchy, the old, aristocratic families of the patrician class, as opposed to the plebeian class of commoners. Patricians saw themselves as descendants of the first 100 men chosen by Romulus as Rome's original senators. As well as holding political power in the Senate, Rome's parliament, the patricians dominated economic life, too, through their ownership of vast and extremely profitable estates and plantations. If anything was guaranteed to anger Rome's landowning aristocracy, it was the suggestion they might redistribute some of their holdings among their fellow countrymen.

This is exactly what the tribune Tiberius Gracchus did in 134 BCE. Like Cleisthenes in Athens, he was a high-born aristocrat. He was also a leading light of the reformist Populares faction in the Senate. The Populares were concerned about the growing social inequalities in Rome, with the patricians, represented in the Senate by the Optimates, accumulating more and more wealth at the expense of their low-born plebeian countrymen. Tiberius Gracchus' land reform proposals involved Rome's aristocratic country squires handing over large swathes of their estates to the peasantry. The effect was to inflame the simmering resentment of an aristocracy that did not want to share anything – land, wealth, political power – with a population they despised as an uncouth mass.

The parallels with Athens' experiment with democracy are striking. In both cases a progressive oligarch had the foresight to see that social and economic changes were making their existing forms of government unsustainable, but where Cleisthenes succeeded, Tiberius Gracchus failed. Cleisthenes persuaded enough of his fellow oligarchs it was in their interests to follow his lead; Tiberius Gracchus, on the other hand, was more confrontational. He courted popular support among the plebeians against his fellow oligarchs, and the fiery rhetoric he deployed in the Forum gave the Optimates the excuse they needed to bring him down. Under the guise of saving Rome from a burgeoning tyrant, in 133

Tiberius and Gaius Gracchus, brothers and populist politicians who fell foul of Rome's oligarchic deep state.

BCE Rome's aristocrats, senators and a hired mob of enforcers confronted Tiberius Gracchus and, in the ensuing fight, beat him to death along with 300 of his followers.

In the aftermath of this massacre the Senate actually passed Tiberius Gracchus' reforms – public opinion had swung too far behind the issue to ignore it – but implementation of the act was slow and heavily compromised. In the end, Tiberius Gracchus' radical proposals suffered death by a thousand cuts.

Ten years later this scenario was played out again when Tiberius Gracchus' brother Gaius, also a tribune, tried to force the state to subsidize grain prices in Rome to make it affordable to ordinary citizens. The republic's large landowner and agribusiness deep state disdained this policy. In the inevitable violence that followed, Gaius Gracchus took his own life when cornered by a gang sent by the oligarchs to murder him.

The empire strikes back

What happened to the Gracchi was symptomatic of the state of Roman politics in the waning years of the republic. Before long, the oligarch-dominated Senate would become little more than a talking shop as a cadre of military strongmen emerged that favoured a more direct approach to the exercise of power.

All the offices of state continued as before – senators were appointed, consuls, tribunes and quaestors elected – but they increasingly became proxies for rogue generals pushing their personal agendas. These included Pompey the Great and Julius Caesar, whose bitter power struggle helped to hasten the end of the republic and opened the way for the age of emperors that followed. Both men prioritized military success over politics, so as Rome transitioned from a republic into an empire its deep state morphed from an oligarchic cabal into a military junta.

Augustus, the first emperor, had come to power in 27 BCE on the back of military success. This, and the imperial expansion and influx of wealth that accumulated during his 40-year reign, made his position unassailable. Those who followed were not so fortunate. Augustus' successor, Tiberius, a disillusioned and dissolute old man by the end of his 22-year reign in 37 CE, was supposedly helped on his way to the afterlife by the commander of the Praetorian Guard, Naevius Sutorius Macro. The Praetorian Guard had been established by Augustus as the emperor's personal security detail. Given its proximity to ultimate power, it quickly became a deep-state kingmaker, removing and installing emperors at will. It arranged the assassination of Tiberius' successor Caligula in 41 CE, for example, and murdered 13 Roman emperors in total over the course of its history. By the end of Nero's unhappy reign in 68 CE, Rome's military deep state abandoned all pretence of impartiality and went to war with itself. The year 69 CE saw no fewer than four emperors, all of them military generals. The last of these was Vespasian, commander of Rome's eastern legions, who re-established peace and security.

For the next 400 years, until the final fall of Rome in 476 CE, the majority of the empire's rulers were drawn from the military – but not all of them. When the emperor Commodus (r. 177–92 CE) became violently unhinged towards the end of his rule he was strangled in his bath and replaced by the soldier-politician Pertinax. His two-month reign as emperor ended when he tried to introduce legislation limiting the power of the Praetorian Guard. It reacted by having him assassinated and sold the emperorship off to the highest bidder. The winner, Didius Julianus, was emperor for 65 days before he too was murdered in favour of another military leader, Septimius Severus.

During the so-called 'Imperial Crisis' of 235–284 CE, a period of intense political instability beginning with the rule of Maximinus Thrax, there were 27 different rulers in 49 years. They were known as the 'Barracks Emperors' as most were drawn from the Roman legions. From a supporting role at the inception of the empire, being the tools of ambitious statesmen such as Pompey, Caesar and Augustus, Rome's army quickly became at first the power behind

Septimius Severus, (r. 193–211 CE), one of Rome's more long-lasting military leaders-turned emperor.

the throne and then the power *on* the throne – a deep state no longer but the state itself.

It is ironic, perhaps, that the institutions the military deep state subverted so successfully and for so long outlasted the men

19

that corrupted it. When Rome fell in 476 CE its armies had long since been decimated by successive waves of barbarian invaders. But the Senate remained, and did so until at least 603, when the last recorded mention of it appears.

IMPERIAL JAPAN

For a country where respect for authority is embedded in the culture, Japan has a surprisingly long history of deep-state dissent – emanating, even more surprisingly, from the armed forces. It goes back to 1853, when an American armed fleet arrived in Tokyo Bay and forced the hitherto closed country to open up to international trade. The USA and UK in particular had already begun to exploit the riches of China and Japan was next on their list. This 'invasion' incensed many Japanese, particularly a class of patriotic young men calling themselves the *shishi* ('warriors of high aspiration'). Throughout the 1860s and 1870s they carried out a campaign of assassination and terrorism designed to drive out the Westerners and topple the weak and dishonourable government. Before long, *shishi* sentiment began to infiltrate Japan's armed forces and this, coupled with a change in the country's military organization, led to the creation of a debilitating deep state.

Military manoeuvres

Japan reluctantly engaged more with the world after America's act of gunboat diplomacy in 1853, sending trade envoys to the USA, for example, and diplomatic missions to England. Fatefully, Japan also dispatched army observers to Prussia, Europe's pre-eminent military power. The result was that by 1878 Japan's armed forces had been reorganized entirely along Prussian lines. This included the setting up of a Prussian-style General Staff and, importantly, embracing the Prussian concept of *Kommandogewalt* ('prerogative of supreme command'). This placed the armed forces under the direct control of the emperor, rather than parliament. As Japan's emperor was just a figurehead, the 'supreme prerogative', as it came to be known, turned the armed forces into a de facto autonomous power, and one that was permeated by *shishi*-influenced xenophobia, ultra-nationalism and anti-government sentiment.

To make the military's position even stronger, a quirk in Japan's constitution stated that the prime minister must resign if he couldn't fill all of his cabinet posts. The constitution also decreed that the cabinet positions of army and navy ministers had to be occupied by serving military officers. This meant that the armed forces could bring down the government at any time by simply ordering the army or navy minister to resign. This handed the military deep state a sword of Damocles that it happily dangled over successive prime ministers.

The first test of the supreme prerogative's robustness came in 1895, when the Imperial Army staged a coup in Korea without the authorization or even the knowledge of Japan's government. It was a particularly barbarous operation during which Korea's queen was hacked to death. When the coup commander Lieutenant General Miura Gorō returned to Japan to stand trial for murder the judiciary dutifully followed the General Staff's suggestion to go easy on the 'over-zealous' officer. Astonishingly, the case was dismissed due to lack of evidence – even though the King of Korea himself had watched Gorō lead the assault.

'Black ops' such as Gorō's became a feature of Japanese politics for the next 50 years and revealed a fault line in the country's military deep state. Everyone on either side of the line wanted the same thing, namely the creation of a Pacific-wide Japanese militarized empire, but differed on how to get there. Radicals such as Gorō wanted to seize power and embark on their imperial mission immediately. Conservatives, represented by the General Staff, preferred to work behind the scenes, building towards a strategic pre-emptive strike against their greatest regional rival, the USA. Only then would they seize power and conquer the Pacific. Much of the 1920s and 1930s was consumed by deep-state in-fighting between these factions. Ultimately, the conservatives

Miura Gorō not only escaped punishment for his coup attempt in Korea but was feted as a hero by Japanese nationalists.

emerged triumphant, in Japan at least; in China it was another story.

Imperial ambitions

Manchuria, in eastern China, is rich in coal and minerals, which is why in 1905 Japan defeated Russia in a war for control of the region; China itself was too weak at the time to resist foreign incursions. The force responsible for this victory was known as the Kwantung Army, and from its Manchurian power base it developed into a state within a state, acting with complete independence not just from the Japanese government but from the General Staff, too. In 1928 and 1931 it launched unsanctioned attacks on China and became the most expansionist and nationalistic arm of Japan's military. The Kwantung Army was also the training ground for Japan's most implacable commanders during World War II, notably Hideki Tōjō and Seishirō Itagaki, both of whom would be executed for war crimes in 1948.

Japan's General Staff had more success dealing with military freelancers closer to home, stifling two coups by the radical Cherry Blossom Society in 1931. To show the government who wielded true power, the General Staff tried the coup plotters in a military rather than a civil court, sentencing the ringleader to just 20 days' house arrest for what was essentially an act of treason. Following another coup attempt in 1936, this time by the army's Imperial Way Faction, the General Staff decided to clean house. The world economy was in recession, fascism was spreading in Europe and war was in the air. Japan's deep state knew its time was coming and needed to be ready. It purged the Imperial Way and other radicals from its ranks and then turned its attention to parliament.

In 1937, the armed forces supported the appointment of the popular but ineffective Fumimaro Konoe as Japan's prime minister. This gave the General Staff a free rein. Barely a month after Konoe took office, the army embarked on a massive attack on China and then finalized preparations for total war in the Pacific. When

Japan launched its surprise attack on the US naval base at Pearl Harbor on 7 December 1941, the military had virtually taken over the government.

But Japan's empire never materialized. In gaining control of the state, the military overreached itself. Its fanatical imperialism led to Japan's total defeat in 1945, the dissolution of its armed forces, and the horrors of Hiroshima and Nagasaki.

THE LATE OTTOMAN EMPIRE

Turkey is literally the home of the deep state. The term is a translation of the Turkish phrase *derin devlet* and was first used in the 1990s to describe underhand political manoeuvrings among civil servants, army officers and organized crime (see p.94). But Turkey's deep state extends further back, to the mid-19th century, when the country was the home base of the Ottoman Empire, an imperial power in decline. In this instance, the deep state was less a malign force than a movement aimed at national renewal – which ultimately happened, but not quite how the deep state's leaders intended.

Rise of the Young Ottomans

By the 1860s, the Ottoman Empire was more than 500 years old and feeling its age. Rival imperial powers such as Britain, France and Russia were eyeing Ottoman-held territories such as Egypt, North Africa and the Black Sea, while nationalist groups in the empire were agitating for independence in the Balkans and the Middle East.

Back in the empire's heartland of Turkey, in 1865 a group of six concerned civil servants met for a picnic in Constantinople's Belgrade Forest. By the end of the al fresco meal they had formed what became known as the Patriotic Alliance and had dedicated themselves to arresting the Ottoman Empire's decline. They also swore to rebuild their society along more liberal but also Islamic lines. Eventually, these hard-to-reconcile aims would tear the group apart, but at the time they were a rallying point for disaffected subjects living under the autocratic rule of Sultan Abdülaziz.

As the Patriotic Alliance grew its name changed to the Young Ottomans, a soubriquet that better reflected its members' youthful enthusiasm and imperial loyalty. Early on, the group attracted an influential and well-placed sympathizer: Prince Murad, Abdülaziz's nephew and a future sultan. In him, the Young Ottomans had a highly placed operative inside the sultan's court. They were now officially a deep state.

Namik Kemal was one of the six Belgrade Forest picnickers. He owned the newspaper *Tasvir-i efkâr* ('Picture of Ideas') and used it to advance a pro-reform agenda. Kemal's paper was not shut down by the government, which prompted a slew of more radical periodicals to emerge, including *Ulum* ('Science'), *Inkilab* ('Revolution') and *Ibret* ('Lesson'). But in 1867 the Young Ottomans pushed their luck too far when they published an open letter in *Tasvir-i efkâr* demanding parliamentary democracy. A government crackdown resulted in most of the Young Ottomans fleeing to Paris, where they regrouped around Mustafa Fazil Pasha, an exiled Egyptian dissident. A wealthy scion of Egypt's old royal family, Pasha helped to finance a new radical newspaper called *Hürriyet* ('Freedom'). The deep state was down but not out.

The Young Ottomans' war of attrition paid off in 1871, when Mustafa Fazil Pasha was recalled to Constantinople and appointed justice minister. The Young Ottomans now had a prince inside the imperial palace and a patron in the Ministry of Justice. This should have been their moment, but with the prospect of real power and influence tantalizingly close the Young Ottomans began to fall out. Some favoured building on the political advances they had made and others thought it was time to seize power; one faction wanted to impose an Islamic state while another would only accept a secular republic.

It took the Young Ottomans five years to resolve their differences. In the meantime, a stock market crash followed by unpopular tax increases had weakened Sultan Abdülaziz, as had nationalist revolts in the Balkans and Bulgaria. In May 1876 the Young Ottomans joined a *coup d'état* led by Midhat Pasha, the country's most reform-minded politician. Abdülaziz was deposed and replaced by the crypto-Young Ottoman Prince Murad. Namik Kemal was made a palace secretary, as was Ziya Pasha, one of the driving forces behind *Hürriyet*. The deep state had triumphed.

From Young Ottomans to Young Turks

But the Young Ottomans were nothing if not unlucky. Six days after being deposed, Abdülaziz was found dead in mysterious circumstances. Although suicide was the official verdict, many Turks thought he had been murdered by his usurpers. This damaged the new regime's credibility less than a week after its inception. Worse still, Murad, a mentally unstable alcoholic, had to be removed from power just three months into his reign. His replacement was the far more authoritarian Abdül Hamid II. By early 1878 Abdül Hamid had regained political power from parliament and rescinded the liberal constitution that the coup plotters had instigated.

Yet where the Young Ottomans failed, the so-called Young Turks of a generation later succeeded. Their careers mirrored almost exactly those of their Young Ottoman predecessors. For a start, they were similarly exiled to Paris, in the Young Turks' case following a failed 1889 plot to remove the conservative and inflexible Abdül Hamid II. Also, like the Young Ottomans, they were split ideologically between the nationalist Committee of Union and Progress (CUP) that favoured centralized government, and the League of Private Initiative and Decentralization (LPID), which was more federally-minded. Also like the Young Ottomans, the Young Turks waged a propaganda war against Abdül Hamid II's regime through newspapers such as *Meşveret* ('Consultation'). In the final analysis, however, the Young Turks succeeded where the Young Ottomans failed because of their support among the army.

In the first decade of the 1900s, external pressures were threatening the Ottoman Empire like never before as independence movements in the Middle East and south-east Europe gathered momentum and the prospect of a world war grew ever closer. Under pressure from the army, Abdül Hamid II was forced to reinstate the constitution he had revoked in 1878, effectively handing power over to the Young Turks' CUP faction in 1908. Following a feeble counter-coup attempt in 1909, Abdül Hamid II was deposed in favour of his more amenable brother, Mehmed. The so-called Young Turk Revolution was complete.

Disastrously, the Young Turks' Ottoman Empire sided with Germany in World War I. At the end of the conflict in 1918, vast chunks of the empire were hived off, Constantinople was occupied by foreign troops and the Young Turks' regime was in disarray. This opened the way for the more authoritarian World War I hero Mustafa Kemal to grab power in 1923. Renamed Atatürk ('father of the Turks') by his supporters, he dissolved the Ottoman Empire,

Lithograph celebrating the Young Turk revolution of 1908. The angel holds a banner bearing the words 'freedom, equality, brotherhood'.

27

declared Turkey a republic and had himself appointed president, a position he held unopposed until his death in 1938.

The politics and culture of the nation that Atatürk created are still in place today, with its tradition of authoritarian rule and an uneasy secularism in a predominantly Islamic region. While the deep state helped to end the Ottoman Empire, it did not long survive it – at least not in its liberal form. Today, modern Turkey has a different kind of deep state operating within its borders, as we shall see in Chapter 3.

GERMANY'S CATHOLIC DEEP STATE

In 1862, the great statesman Otto von Bismarck was appointed prime minister of Prussia and he arrived in office with a plan: the unification of all German-speaking states into a single nation. This naturally ruffled the feathers of France, unnerved at the idea of a German superstate on its doorstep, and on 19 July 1870 Emperor Napoleon III of France declared war on Prussia, expecting a swift and decisive victory. His expectations were more than met – by Prussia. When the French army was comprehensively defeated at the Battle of Sedan in September 1870 the road lay open for Bismarck to enact his political project, and in January 1871 a Prussian-controlled German Empire was declared in the Hall of Mirrors in Versailles.

As chancellor of the new nation, a position he held until 1890, Bismarck became Europe's most powerful politician. Having created Germany, he had to unite it. To do this, he needed to identify an enemy within and direct the feelings of his fellow Germans against it – and he found it in the shape of the Catholic Church. The war Bismarck waged against Catholicism offers an interesting insight into how deep states can be convenient fall guys when governments have an agenda to push.

Forging a new nation

In 1866, Protestant Prussia had gone to war against Catholic Austria in a regional power struggle that saw other Germanic

Otto von Bismarck, mastermind of German unification and the country's chancellor from 1871 to 1890.

Catholic states such as Bavaria side with their co-religionists. As those Catholic states were now part of the unified German Empire, a tension had been created that needed to be addressed. In addition, many of Germany's Catholics were not necessarily German. Part of its peace settlement with France in 1871 involved Germany's acquisition of the eastern French region of Alsace-Lorraine. While this was an area rich in iron ore deposits, it also landed Germany with 1.2 million French-speaking Catholics. Eastern Germany, meanwhile, contained some 3 million Catholic Poles. After German unification, around 36 per cent of the population was Catholic, amounting to 15 million souls.

Bismarck's plan was to mould Germany in Protestant Prussia's image, which meant going head to head with the Catholic Church. Fortunately, just when Bismarck needed a *casus belli*, he realized that Pope Pius IX in Rome had already handed him one when he introduced the doctrine of Papal Infallibility in 1870. This decree effectively told Catholics everywhere that they now served two masters – their head of state and the head of their church. This allowed Bismarck to launch what became known as the *Kulturkampf* ('culture struggle') against the Catholic Church's vested interests and build a new nation where Prussian-style government was the supreme and only authority.

In order to pass the necessary legislation to do this, the arch-conservative Bismarck held his nose and made an alliance with Germany's Liberal Party. This was a masterstroke. Bismarck knew that the secular Liberals would happily support his anti-Catholic campaign – and bear the brunt of any conservative backlash afterwards. The chancellor's principal human shield during this process was the Liberal Party's Adalbert Falk, the fiercely anti-clerical minister for religion, education and health and the man who oversaw the passing of the 22 new laws of the *Kulturkampf.*

The process began in the summer of 1871, when responsibility for church-state relations was taken away from Catholic administrators and handed over to Protestant bureaucrats. Following that, anti-

Catholic legislation came in wave after wave. The *Kanzelparagraph* (the Pulpit Law) of November 1871 made criticism of the government by the clergy, Catholic and Protestant, a criminal offence. This was a sign that the *Kulturkampf* was now being used against all Christian denominations where religious interests came into conflict with those of the state. In early 1872, the country's religious schools were placed under government control. The Jesuits were expelled from the German Empire in July 1872, and diplomatic relations were broken off with the Vatican at the end of the year. In spring 1873 the May Laws were introduced, a series of measures that subjected what was left of the Catholic Church in Germany (and all other religious groups) to complete state control. The *coup de grâce* came in 1875 with the passing of the so-called Breadbasket Bill. This drastic measure dissolved all religious orders in Germany, except those actively engaged in caring for the sick. All church property was confiscated and religious marriage services were banned.

As Catholic anger mounted over the harsh treatment it was joined by Protestant unrest. When Bismarck began receiving complaints from prominent Protestants about the Liberals' over-enthusiastic prosecution of the *Kulturkampf* he decided to wind things down.

Mission accomplished

Bismarck was greatly helped in his tactical manoeuvring by the growing power of the Centre Party, which had been set up in 1870 to protect Catholic interests. In state elections in 1873 the Centre Party almost doubled its representation in the Reichstag from 50 to 90 seats, and its support grew year by year. Bismarck, one of the shrewdest politicians ever, correctly interpreted this as a positive development. It was a sign that Catholic activism was moving away from the churches, the monasteries and the religious schools and into parliament, where it could be better monitored and controlled. It also meant that, once fences could be mended,

Bismarck could ally with the Centre Party and other conservative forces against his erstwhile allies the Liberals. With his political objectives attained, Bismarck began to roll back much of his anti-Catholic legislation little by little and by 1882 diplomatic ties with the Vatican had been restored.

In the meantime, Germany had been 'cleansed' of the hard-to-manage shock-troops of Catholicism: by 1878 more than a quarter of the country's Catholic parish churches lay empty, 1,800 priests had been jailed or exiled for failing to comply with *Kulturkampf* legislation, and almost half of all monks and nuns had left the country. Thousands of laypersons had also been imprisoned for helping the Catholic Church to avoid compliance with the new laws.

In truth, Germany's Catholic deep state had always been more imagined than real. While Catholics certainly had the potential to undermine the new German Empire, they had never shown any inclination to do so. It was Bismarck's clever political calculation that the Catholic Church could be targeted enough to drive its more radical and Rome-facing loyalists away while he encouraged its politically powerful and agreeably conservative adherents to become part of the German state, rather than apart from it.

FRANCE'S THIRD REPUBLIC

France was in turmoil following its defeat in the Franco-Prussian War of 1870–71. The last shot in anger had barely been fired when the citizens of the capital rose up in a radical socialist revolt known as the Paris Commune. Although the Commune lasted just two months, its bloody suppression left an indelible stain on the new Third Republic, which ever-after was known as 'La Gueuse' ('the wench') by its enemies.

At the same time, right-wing elements in France were unsure what the future held, with royalists and Bonapartists agitating for either a restoration of the monarchy or a new Napoleon. Underlying left- and right-wing discontent was resentment over

France's shocking loss to Prussia. This led to a movement known as *revanchism* ('revengism'), the aim of which was to re-engage Prussia in war to regain both the territory and the national pride France had lost.

While it appeared these diverse interests could never be reconciled, in the late 1880s a man came along who thought he knew how to achieve it – and whom the royalists saw as a Trojan horse they could use to trick their way to power.

Le Général Revanche

Georges Boulanger was a general who had fought in the Franco-Prussian War. When he entered politics in the early 1880s, he was a man of the left. He served as war minister in 1886, but by the spring of the following year he had moved significantly to the right, preaching a brand of militaristic populist politics that endeared him to the working classes and earned him the nickname 'Le Général Revanche'. Boulanger's impassioned nationalism also earned him the sack from government in May 1887, after which he set up his own political movement, known as Boulangism.

The country's monarchist elements looked on with interest as Boulanger blazed a trail through French politics. Louis Philippe, the last king of France, had been deposed in 1848, and ever since the country's royalists had longed for a restoration. By the 1880s this meant putting Louis Philippe's grandson, Philippe, Count of Paris, on the throne. Since the inception of the Third Republic in 1871, conservatives and royalists had been systematically squeezed out of legislative and civic positions. With its traditional pathways to power cut off, the royalist deep state knew the only way to recall the Count of Paris from exile in England was to use Boulanger as a proxy.

As good fortune would have it, the royalists knew exactly how to reel in their man. Boulanger's new movement needed finance. In early 1887 Boulanger's friend and confidant Count Arthur Dillon was secretly approached by the Marquis Ludovic de Beauvoir,

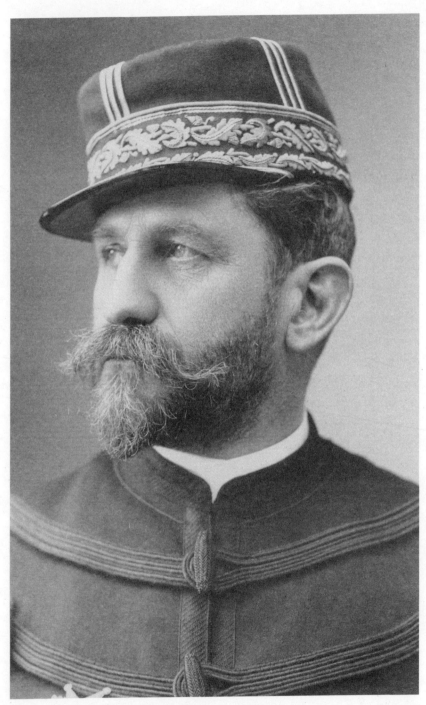

The man who would be king: Georges Boulanger.

the Count of Paris' personal secretary, to see if the general was prepared to cut a deal in return for back-channel royal funding. The answer was an emphatic yes. The agreement that Dillon and de Beauvoir struck was for Boulanger to build up his movement, win the presidency and, once in office, announce an end to the republic and restore the monarchy. In return for staging this surrogate coup Boulanger would be given a senior position in the French army. Although this cast Boulanger as the conspiracy's junior partner he was happy with the arrangement. For all of his bullish charisma and crowd-pleasing rhetoric, Boulanger was an indecisive, ambivalent figure who both craved and feared power, a character trait that would prove to be his downfall.

The deal done, wealthy royalist sympathizers were clandestinely inducted into the plot. One of the keenest donors was the Duchesse d'Uzès. As heiress to the Veuve Cliquot champagne fortune, she could easily afford the three million francs she donated to the Boulangist cause. This was more than matched by Baron Maurice de Hirsch, a financier who placed up to five million francs in the Boulangist coffers. The fact that the pro-Boulanger royalist plot could contain backers as diverse as the deeply conservative and anti-Semitic Duchesse d'Uzès and Hirsch, who was both German and Jewish, speaks volumes about the renegade general's strange appeal.

Once gathered, all funds were handled by a secretive committee headed by the Marquis de Beauvoir, which included conservative notables such as the newspaper magnate Arthur Meyer and the staunchly Catholic politicians Albert de Mun and Jacques Piou. While the committee doled out monies to Boulanger, it also made it clear to him that the tap could be easily turned off if he showed signs of defaulting on his deal.

With illicit royalist money in Boulanger's pocket and conservative newspapers such as Arthur Meyer's *Le Gaulois* promoting him, candidates who supported him won by-election after by-election throughout 1887 and 1888. It appeared that Le Général Revanche had unstoppable momentum and that it was only a matter of time before he either won or took over the state. Everything hinged on the Paris by-election of January 1889, where Boulanger himself stood as a candidate. The French capital was a bastion of left-wing republicanism, the home of the Commune. Up to this point, Boulangism had been popular in traditionally conservative areas such as the countryside and in smaller towns and villages. If Boulanger won Paris, many surmised, the nation was his for the taking.

The end of Boulangism

When Boulanger duly captured the seat with almost a quarter of a million votes (his closest rival garnered 163,000 votes) France held its breath. But, at the crucial moment, Boulanger's vacillating nature got the better of him and he did nothing. The royalists were justifiably furious with Boulanger, but so were his millions of supporters. Almost overnight Boulanger's spell was broken and the people of France woke up. As public opinion turned, the government of prime minister Pierre Tirard struck. Treason charges were laid against the general, who on 1 April 1889 fled to Brussels. When a general election was held that autumn, Boulangist candidates confirmed the movement's death by winning just 12 per cent of the popular vote.

Boulangism was over and the royalists embarked on a hasty cover-up operation. At a surreptitious meeting at the house of the Duchesse d'Uzès, Jacques Piou reminded his co-conspirators their support of Boulanger represented 'material proof of an understanding whose purpose was not an electoral alliance but the overthrow of the government'. Incriminating papers were destroyed and journalists who got too close to the story were paid off. As for Boulanger, never the most stable character, on 30 September 1891 he committed suicide at the graveside of his mistress Madame de Bonnemains in the Ixelles Cemetery in Brussels.

The royalists' deep state role in the Boulanger affair demonstrated the difficulties traditional conservatives experienced in adapting to a changing world of democratic politics, mass media and unbridled populism. Some observers have seen in Boulangism a prototype of Nazism, with a charismatic leader emerging from a war-torn nation and harnessing popular discontent. The parallels certainly extend to both movements' deep-state backers, who in each case mistakenly thought they could control 'their' man. The consequences were damaging for the royalists over Boulanger, but were disastrous in the case of Adolf Hitler some 40 years later, the legacy of whose dictatorship continued long after his suicide in 1945 and reverberate still (see pp.54–60).

CHAPTER 2

EUROPEAN DEEP STATES

THE BIG THEME of Europe's deep states is the role of the bureaucracy. In France and the UK, civil service elites from age-old networks of social privilege manage their nations. It's supposed to be a neutral, benevolent system that stands above politics, but it doesn't entirely do so. In France, deeply entrenched elites move back and forth between the worlds of bureaucracy and politics, blurring the lines between two disciplines best kept separate, while in the UK the relationship between Whitehall mandarins and their political masters is often adversarial, especially when inflamed by divisive issues such as Brexit. In both countries, the deep states have usually been able to combine their twin aims of administering their nations while fighting off any moves by political leaders to introduce reforms that threaten their dominant positions.

Germany, too, has its own public service deep-state problems. After World War II, it found its justice system infiltrated by former Nazis with secrets they needed to protect, and this elided into an intelligence service that in recent times has had an ambivalent relationship with the extreme nationalists and neo-Nazis it is supposed to be monitoring. Meanwhile, in Italy and Russia, state-sponsored webs of criminals, corrupt politicians and dishonest business leaders work together to steal their countries' wealth with impunity.

ITALY

There were deep states in Italy before there was Italy, going back as far as Ancient Rome (see pp.14–20). Until the 1990s, that tradition was continued in a coalition of organized crime, rogue Freemasons, corrupt business leaders and compromised politicians mismanaging the country until the edifice of government finally collapsed.

What emerged from the wreckage was in some respects worse. The old corrupt systems were gone, but at least they had been systems. Italian politics today is much more fluid and improvised than previously. Authoritarian and post-fascist parties are on the rise and trust in politicians is at an all-time low. It's a situation the former deep states – and some new ones – are poised to exploit.

The Boss of Bosses

It was in reaction to one-party Fascist totalitarianism that post-war Italy adopted proportional representation for its electoral system. Yet while Italy's politics after 1945 were notoriously unstable – with just under 70 governments in 75 years, as of 2020 – the Christian Democrats and their leader Giulio Andreotti still managed to dominate the country for much of that period, propped up by several deep-state interests. The most ruthless of these was Sicily's Cosa Nostra. Its deal with the Christian Democrats was simple: in return for a free hand to continue its criminal activities, Palermo's mafiosi ensured healthy Christian Democrat majorities in most Sicilian constituencies, courtesy of rigged ballots and forged votes.

From the late 1960s this arrangement was facilitated by Salvatore Lima, the one-time Christian Democrat mayor of Palermo who acted as the bagman for Giulio Andreotti back in Rome. This was a prestigious position. To his friends, Andreotti was 'Giulio the Divine'; to his many enemies, he was 'Beelzebub', 'The Black Pope' and 'The Hunchback' (because of his stooping posture). In his 50-year career this modern-day Machiavelli held every major office in Italian politics and was prime minister no fewer than seven times.

Their Sicilian-bought votes played a major part in maintaining the Christian Democrats as Italy's biggest party, so it was a disaster for Andreotti when at the beginning of the 1980s his partners in the 'moderate' Palermo mafia were wiped out in a gang war by a rival clan from the town of Corleone, led by Salvatore 'Totò' Riina. Known as 'The Beast', Riina ended the mafia's deal with the Christian Democrats and embarked instead on a campaign of murders, bombings and assassinations designed to terrorize the

Giulio Andreotti, Italy's 'Black Pope', casts his vote in a 1953 election.

state into submission. Deprived of its Sicilian votes, the Christian Democrats lost the 1980 general election to Bettino Craxi's Socialist Party (PSI). The war between the mafia and the Socialist Party-led state that followed culminated in the conviction of 338 mafiosi at a huge 1987 'maxi-trial' in Palermo. Riina, on the run, was given two life sentences *in absentia*.

After lodging an appeal, Riina and his chief lieutenants reopened the Cosa Nostra's back-channel to the Christian Democrats and pressurized Andreotti and Lima to ensure its magistrate of choice, Corrado Carnevale, known as 'The Sentence Killer', oversaw the application to overturn their sentences. This was not forthcoming, and when the original sentences were upheld, Salvatore Lima was murdered by Cosa Nostra hitmen in March 1992. This was followed by the assassinations of Giovanni Falcone and Paolo Borsellino, two high-profile magistrates investigating the mafia.

Although he lived for another 21 years, Andreotti never held high office again following these outrages. In 1993, following the capture of Totò Riina, Andreotti was tried and acquitted of mafia collusion, relying mainly on Italy's statute of limitations to rule his alleged crimes out of bounds. In a parallel legal process, Andreotti was acquitted, after two appeals, of complicity in the 1979 murder of the investigative journalist Mino Pecorelli.

Propaganda Due

Alongside the mafia, Italy's other major post-war deep state was Propaganda Due (P2). Originally a Masonic lodge, it became an illegal secret society in 1976 when it was ejected from the Freemasons' movement because of the crypto-fascist views of its leader, the financier Licio Gelli.

Freed of Masonic control, Gelli reshaped P2 into a shadow state dedicated to opposing communism and suppressing democracy. For more than 30 years, he conspired with a network of like-minded senior politicians, journalists, military leaders, judges and businessmen – one of whom, the Sicilian-born banker Michele 'The

Shark' Sindona, would inadvertently destroy not just P2 but the whole architecture of Italian politics.

Sindona used the banks he owned to launder mafia money, and when several of these banks failed in 1979 following a financial crash, investigators uncovered evidence of criminal activity. They also unearthed a suspicious 'commission' payment of US$5.6 million to Archbishop Paul Marcinkus, president of the Vatican Bank, and Roberto Calvi, the head of Banco Ambrosiano, a man known as 'God's banker' due to his close ties to the papacy. Once the alleged links between the mafia, Sindona, the Vatican and Calvi emerged, things unravelled quickly. By 1982 Banco Ambrosiano had collapsed and Roberto Calvi, on the run from Italian justice, was found hanged under Blackfriars Bridge in London. As Calvi and Michele Sindona were both members of P2 its offices were raided and incriminating papers recovered, including a blueprint for a right-wing coup entitled 'Plan for a Democratic Rebirth'. A list of almost 1,000 P2 members was also found, featuring the names of the heads of all three branches of Italy's secret services and that of Silvio Berlusconi, the media tycoon and future Italian prime minister.

From here, the net widened to cover a nationwide system of corruption that Italians dubbed 'Tangentopoli' ('Bribesville') and, in 1992, the magistrate Antonio di Pietro was appointed to oversee a probe into it known as 'Mani Pulite' ('Clean Hands'). In time, 5,000 public figures were investigated and more than 400 corrupt civic councils dissolved. Judges were arrested, 80 financial regulators were questioned and 300 business leaders were charged with corruption thought to be worth US$4 billion annually. The Bribesville scandal epitomized the Italian concept of *dietrologia* ('behindology'), the search for hidden, usually nefarious, motives behind official state acts. When questioned, PSI leader Bettino Craxi admitted that 'everyone was doing this' and that corruption and collusion was 'the price of politics'. In the public outcry that followed Craxi fled to Tunisia, where he remained until his death in 2000.

The Clean Hands investigation decimated Italy's political establishment. Both the Christian Democrat and PSI parties collapsed, taking the remains of the Bribesville-inspired deep state with them and leaving Silvio Berlusconi's Forza Italia party, formed in 1994, as the main beneficiary of the reshaped political landscape. Forza Italia was in and out of government for the next 20 years, despite, or regardless of, Berlusconi's many brushes with the law for corruption and other offences.

Today, Italy's politics are more fractious than ever, with unstable governments, post-fascist political parties and the populist Five Star Movement advocating a kind of make-it-up-as-you-go-along politics that will lead who knows where. In this situation, it may not be long before Italians grow nostalgic for the guiding hand of its old deep states once more.

FRANCE

France's deep state has existed for 200 years. In each generation it searches out the brightest and the best and subjects them to a gruelling training regime that only the fittest survive. But it's not a special ops unit or an undercover intelligence division – it's more powerful than that. It's the civil service.

Not all of the civil service, of course. France's administrative deep state comprises at most a couple of thousand souls, drawn from a handful of exclusive schools and universities. Its members glide effortlessly between the worlds of bureaucracy, politics and business, building networks and forging links that outsiders cannot penetrate. Until recently, France's administrative deep state reigned supreme, but now its reluctance to change is causing France to fall behind in a globalizing, socially mobile and competitive world.

A false start

France presents itself as classless, meritocratic – the land of *liberté, egalité, fraternité* (liberty, equality, fraternity). Where you went to school or university, for example, should not matter – but it does.

In fact, France operates an elitist education system that is engineered to guarantee a select few the membership of an exclusive shadow government.

It starts early. France's schools are free, with entrance based on educational merit, but even so the most prestigious institutions such as the Lycée Henri-IV, École Jeannine Manuel and the Lycée Louis-le-Grand remain filled with students whose parents are overwhelmingly affluent, white and well-connected. The most able of these students are singled out and, on reaching the school-leaving age of 18, guided away from university and directed instead toward taking the two-year preparatory classes, or *prépas*, for entrance into one of the *grandes écoles*. These are the colleges that train the country's future leaders, grooming them for entry into the administrative deep state. There are around 200 *grandes écoles*, but it's the 'big five' that really count: the public service-

Paris' École nationale d'administration, *France's most prestigious finishing school for presidents and prime ministers.*

focused *Institut d'études politiques de Paris* (known as Sciences Po); the humanities-based *École normale supérieure* (ENS); the HEC Paris business school; the *École polytechnique* (or, simply, 'X'), specializing in science and technology; and the *École nationale d'administration* (ENA), the school for future senior civil service and governing elites. Of these five, X and ENA are the most prestigious.

French presidents Valéry Giscard d'Estaing, Jacques Chirac, François Hollande and Emmanuel Macron are all *énarques*, as ENA alumni are known, as have been seven French prime ministers to date. ENA and X respectively produce around 100 and 400 graduates annually, just 0.057 per cent of the total graduate population. On leaving college, virtually every one of them takes a high-status job in one of the most exclusive civil service departments. From there, they move back and forth between the interlinked worlds of civil service, politics and business, trying on each sector for size to find the best fit. In a 1990s survey, 84 per cent of board members from France's top 40 companies were *grandes écoles* graduates; today, 60 per cent of the CEOs of France's largest 100 businesses attended a *grande école*.

This process has been operating since the first *grandes écoles* opened in the mid-1700s. It made sense then, when mass education did not exist, literacy rates were low and social mobility was an impossible dream. In the modern world, despite occasional concessions to affirmative action and modernization, the *grandes écoles* appear anachronistic, their graduates gaining more from attending them than the nation does from the careers those graduates go on to forge.

One rule for the rich

Eventually, it took a disaffected product of the system to try to change it. A Sciences Po dropout, Nicolas Sarközy portrayed himself as a political outsider. When he was elected president in 2007, it was on a platform of economic liberalism and administrative reform. This alarmed the elite deep state, whose instincts were more corporatist than those of the free market champion Sarközy. The deep state's response to Sarközy's call for change shows both how it exercised its hegemony and what it was prepared to do when its power came under threat.

One of the reasons the French elite deep state is so successful is because of a long tradition of state intervention in the economy and industry. Known as *dirigisme*, it's a curious hybrid of UK-style nationalization, Soviet planning and competitive capitalism. From the end of World War II until the global oil crisis of the mid-1970s, it gave France what historians call *les trentes glorieuses* ('the 30 glorious years'), when civil servants, politicians and business leaders – drawn overwhelmingly from *grandes écoles*-educated elites – worked together to oversee the country's booming economy. Some major firms, such as Renault, were taken into state ownership, while others were supported with tax breaks, subsidies and public investment. It was a win-win for the elite deep state. Its members got to monopolize the well-paid and influential jobs, and France thrived.

However, as the world changed, France's deep state didn't. It struggled to cope with the free-market liberalism of the 1980s and the globalization that developed from the 1990s onwards. The state ownership or partial control of large corporations made them uncompetitive. In 2003, for example, France Telecom was excluded from bidding on the lucrative contracts to restore post-Gulf War Iraq's mobile phone networks because it was part-owned by the French government.

Nicolas Sarközy wanted to change all that. France was falling behind, he said, and the *grandes écoles* system created a ruling elite that took care of its own but was out of touch with the needs of ordinary French people. He became known as 'Nicolas the American', after his advocacy of US-style neo-liberal, market-driven policies. But this was apostasy for the *dirigiste* deep state. As soon as he became president in 2007, Sarközy found his legislative programme blocked, watered down or ignored by France's bureaucrats. A Sarközy plan to abolish 150,000 civil service jobs, for example, resulted in tens of thousands *more* jobs being created. The global economic crisis of 2008 only further convinced the interventionist and protectionist elite deep state that its policies were right and Sarközy's were wrong. Before long, accusations began to circulate of corruption in Sarközy's government and illegal campaign funding, chipping away at his popularity and destroying his credibility.

When Sarközy was defeated in the 2012 presidential election France's elites breathed a sigh of relief, especially as his replacement was the Socialist Party's François Hollande. While Sarközy was a Sciences Po drop-out, Hollande did not just complete Sciences Po but went on to HEC Paris and ENA too. From there he joined the *Cour des comptes*, the powerful government auditing agency seen as the holy of holies for ambitious *grandes écoles* graduates. In short, Hollande was the archetypal administrative deep state avatar.

'Help! The énarques are back' was a headline in *Le Figaro* magazine when Hollande became president. Around 60 per cent of officials in his administration were X or ENA alumni, including several members of Hollande's own 1980 ENA graduation class – one of whom was his ex-partner, Ségolène Royal. 'We always see each other a lot, we spend holidays together, New Year's Eve,' he said of his former *grandes écoles* colleagues in a 1988 interview. 'Our children know each other. Has this helped our careers? It is above all a friendly bond that allowed us to stay strong when things were not going well.'

Ironically, things did not go well for François Hollande's presidency. His elite deep-state attachment to outdated, France-focused *dirigiste* policies in a globalizing world meant that he was unequipped or unwilling to deal with the country's social and economic issues. Frustrated by their inability to break into the charmed circle of *grandes écoles* elites, many ambitious French people have simply moved on. California's Silicon Valley is now

47

Nicolas Sarközy in 2010, at the height of his unsuccessful campaign to reform what he saw as France's outdated bureaucracy.

home to almost 60,000 digitally oriented French citizens, and, before Brexit at least, there were at least 120,000 French nationals living in the UK, the majority in London. With no viable answers to France's problems, Hollande did not even stand for re-election in 2017, and the presidency was won by his former protégé Emmanuel Macron, now leading the La Republique En Marche! party – a political grouping Macron carefully describes as progressive rather than left-wing, right-wing or centrist.

Macron's establishment credentials were impeccable: Lycée Henri-IV, Sciences Po, ENA, civil service mandarin, investment banker with Rothschild & Cie. But despite being an administrative deep-state man to his very bones, Macron also shared Nicolas Sarközy's enthusiasm for market-based solutions to France's problems over the cozy paternalism of the past. His introduction of tax breaks for the wealthy and the imposition of a regressive fuel tax earned him the nickname 'the president of the rich' and brought protesters on to the streets in the *gilet jaunes* ('yellow jacket') movement beginning in late 2018. Macron was so alarmed by the *gilet jaunes* anti-establishment vehemence that he briefly floated the idea of closing down ENA. But Macron's *grandes écoles* training soon kicked in and, like Hollande, he responded to criticism by surrounding himself in government with contemporaries from his 2004 ENA graduation class who shared his scepticism of the *dirigiste* consensus. He then prepared himself for a fight on two fronts: against the protesting citizens, who wanted jobs and opportunities, and against the *grandes écoles* traditionalists who saw Macron as a dangerous neo-conservative and a threat to their deep state privileges.

In 1789, the people of France revolted to overthrow their monarch and aristocracy. While it's unlikely their modern-day equivalents of president and elite deep state are in similarly mortal danger, the disconnect between France's rulers and ruled is growing and will be unfixable until the elite deep state fixes itself.

RUSSIA

It is said that democracy would not work in Russia – but how could we know? It's never been tried. Centuries of tsarist autocracy was followed from 1917 by decades of Marxist totalitarianism. The collapse of the Soviet system in 1991 meant that Russia finally had the opportunity to give power to its people. They are still waiting. And while they wait, a deep-state kleptocracy of former secret servicemen, public officials and oligarchs has been helping itself to the nation's riches, watched over by Russia's head of state, Vladimir Putin.

Sale of the century

Boris Yeltsin was Russia's first post-Soviet president and his primary task in office was to stabilize the country's collapsing economy. The method he applied was 'shock therapy', the fast and cheap selling of state-owned assets. The problem was that only two groups in the early 1990s had the funds to buy what was on offer: former KGB operatives recently flush with illegally acquired funds from the defunct Communist Party and the tiny emerging class of putative oligarchs from the 'grey economy' – that part of Russian business life occupying the shadowy hinterland between the black market and legitimate commerce. Between them, both parties snapped up huge enterprises such as Novolipetsk Steel and the oil companies Yukos, Sibneft and Lukoil for a fraction of their true value.

The KGB cash came from an especially interesting source. From the 1970s the Soviet Union's ruling Communist Party sold Russian oil and Ukrainian grain overseas, secreting the money in offshore accounts to fund secret service operations. When the Communist Party disappeared in 1991 no one was left in authority to claim the money, so a cohort of KGB officers took the hundreds of millions of dollars, quit their jobs and reinvented themselves as business tycoons. Ambitious KGB agents without access to the black-ops slush fund offered their services instead to the soon-to-be oligarchs as front men with government connections to help them purchase state-owned businesses or trade on the newly established stock exchange – which, according to the Russian magazine *Stolitsa* in 1991, was two-thirds comprised of ex-KGB officers. By the mid-1990s, the oligarchs had become the most successful beneficiaries of Boris Yeltsin's largesse, with men such as Boris Berezovsky, Vladimir Vinogradov and Mikhail Khodorkovsky owning up to 70 per cent of Russia's wealth. By the end of the decade they were coalescing into an oligarchic deep state. But, at the last minute, everything changed when Boris Yeltsin unexpectedly resigned on 31 December 1999 and was replaced by Russia's prime minister, Vladimir Putin.

Jobs for the boys

Putin was, and remains, a KGB man. He joined the service in 1975 and only left in 1991 when the Soviet Union was abolished. Like many of his former comrades, he prospered during the 'gold rush' of the early 1990s, entering politics instead of business and working for Anatoly Sobchak, his university law professor and mayor of St Petersburg. From there, Putin transferred to Boris Yeltsin's presidential office, becoming deputy prime minister, head of the FSB (which replaced the KGB in 1995), prime minister and then president.

In his early days with Sobchak, Putin was implicated in a food-for-oil bribery scandal, after which an official inquiry recommended his firing. Putin survived, and, if the subsequent allegations against him are accurate, brought his talent for political manoeuvring and financial wrongdoing into the presidential palace. First, though, Putin had to deal with the oligarchs. They were given two choices: share their spoils or face the consequences. Those that refused, such as Boris Berezovsky, were driven into exile (to the UK, where he died in unexplained circumstances in 2013) or, like the oil trader Mikhail Khodorkovsky in 2005, imprisoned on possibly fabricated charges. Unsurprisingly, the remaining oligarchs pledged their allegiance and paid their tithes.

Putin then set about creating a deep state of his own, centred around his old secret service colleagues. Almost one-third of government officials during Putin's first presidential term from 2000–8 were ex-KGB and FSB *siloviki* (literally 'men of force'). One of Putin's longest-lasting *siloviki* is Sergei Ivanov. He and Putin served in the same KGB unit from 1975 to 1991 and Ivanov has since held several high political offices, including deputy prime minister, allowing him to amass power and riches for himself and his family. Ivanov's son, Sergei Jr, was appointed to the boards of several large Russian corporations while still in his 20s and in 2017, aged 36, was made chief executive of the state-run diamond mining company, Alrosa, which produces around one-quarter of the world's diamonds.

MONEY TALKS

Not all of Putin's close associates are former spooks, though. Vladimir Yakunin was a diplomat who owned a dacha (country home) in the same gated community as Putin in the early 1990s. In 2005, Yakunin landed the plum job of president of the state-owned Russian Railways. Over the next 10 years the company handed out billions of dollars for non-existent services to fake contractors. According to a Reuters investigation, during the period 2010–13, railway contracts worth US$340 million were awarded in bid processes where only two companies took part, both of which were set up on the same day by the same person acting for an undisclosed owner. In his final year in post, Yakunin presided over a US$1.6 billion loss, the result of 'corruption and mismanagement', according to the Russian opposition politician and anti-graft campaigner Alexey Navalny.

The cost of corruption in Russia is estimated at US$300 billion. Capital flight – the exporting of the country's wealth – has seen US$350 billion leave Russia since 2005. Today, just over 100 billionaires control 35 per cent of Russia's wealth, and the secret service deep state, with Putin at its head, takes a share of it all.

Putin's right-hand man? Russia's most influential siloviki, *Sergei Ivanov.*

Estimates of Vladimir Putin's personal wealth vary. The financier Bill Browder, once the largest portfolio investor in Russia, told a US Senate Judiciary Committee in 2017 it was US$200 billion. Other estimates put it at US$70 billion. Either way, it massively trumps the average Russian income of US$800 a month in a country where 21 million people, 14 per cent of the population, live in poverty. Meanwhile, stolen state cash is laundered through Cyprus then transferred to offshore companies in tax havens such as the British Virgin Islands or Gibraltar. Typically, 'cleaned' money is then invested in London's luxury housing market, artificially inflating already high property prices.

The rise of the kleptocratic deep state under Vladimir Putin has coincided with an increase in the country's illicit activities abroad to undermine and destabilize its international rivals. Russia's secret service interference in the US 2016 presidential election is well known (see pp.211–12), as is its fomenting of unrest in Ukraine in 2014, all, and more, funded in part by back-channel deep-state cash. None of this, surely, is what Boris Yeltsin had in mind when he handed presidential power to Vladimir Putin on New Year's Eve in 1999 and asked him to 'take care of Russia'.

GERMANY

Given Germany's 20th-century history, any suggestion of right-wing activity there since 1945 is monitored with interest. Yet that monitoring has not been rigorous enough, since for decades extreme nationalist and ex- and Neo-Nazi groups have exercised a pervasive impact on the country through its judiciary and its intelligence services. Given Germany's reputation as a post-war beacon of responsible, socially liberal and progressive politics, it's testament to the right-wing deep state's ability to wield influence while lying low.

New roles for Nazis

When discussing the fate of post-war Nazis, the focus is often on the complicity of highly placed Vatican priests and National Socialist sympathizers in helping war criminals escape Europe for new lives in South America, especially when those who fled included figures such as Dr Joseph Mengele, Auschwitz's 'Angel of Death', and Adolf Eichmann, one of the organizers of the Holocaust. But, from a deep-state perspective, concentrating on these 'ratlines' lets off the hook the tens of thousands of Nazis, including SS members and war criminals, who remained in Germany – especially those who went on to take important roles in public life to protect themselves and their former comrades from any form of reckoning. This was made easier for them by the Soviet Union's installation of a puppet regime in East Germany at the end of World War II. The West German chancellor, Konrad Adenauer, argued that he needed experienced Nazi-era managers and administrators in his government to ensure his country constituted a strong barrier against the further spread of communism. When his own chief of staff, Hans Globke, was revealed in 1950 to have helped draft the racist Nuremberg Laws under Hitler, Adenauer kept him in post.

Adenauer's reasoning made sense, but it opened the way for systemic abuse and the CIA was happy to oblige. With West German government approval, the American spy agency funded and set up an intelligence agency known as the Gehlen Organization (or, simply, the Org) to repel Soviet attempts at infiltration and espionage. The Org was headed by Major General Reinhard Gehlen, the former chief of Nazi military intelligence on the Eastern Front. Under Gehlen, the Org recruited scores of former Nazis, including, it is alleged, war criminals such as the SS officers Alois Brunner, accused of the deaths of 100,000 Jews in the Holocaust, and Karl Silberbauer, the man who arrested Anne Frank.

In 1956 the Org became the Federal Intelligence Service (or BND, *Bundesnachrichtendienst*), West Germany's equivalent of the CIA or Britain's MI6. Reinhard Gehlen remained in post until 1968, as did many other Nazis, including Gerhard Wessel, Gehlen's replacement as director. From there, the far right's

Former Nazi Reinhard Gehlen enjoyed a long post-war career heading up West Germany's CIA-funded anti-Soviet counter-intelligence agency.

penetration of the secret services became a constant in post-war German history.

Justice denied

While former SS officers and war criminals were inserting themselves into the intelligence hierarchy, an even more elite company of one-time Nazis was taking over West Germany's legal system. Between 1949 and the early 1970s, for example, 90 of the 170 highest-ranking justice ministry officials had been Nazi Party members – a higher proportion than had been the case during the Third Reich. One of these men was Franz Massfeller, a senior jurist in the family law division. In the Nazi era he had helped to write the anti-Semitic Law for the Protection of Blood and Honour and later oversaw the introduction of legislation outlawing mixed marriages between Jews and non-Jews.

The justice ministry's ex-Nazi deep state became adept at not drawing attention to itself, operating a policy they called 'crow justice': if you don't peck out my eyes, I won't peck out yours. Safe in their anonymity, these men were thereafter free to deny post-war justice to surviving victims of the Nazis. In 1958 the deep-state-dominated justice ministry issued an amnesty for Nazi war criminals. Two years later it decreed that the statute of limitations for prosecuting war crimes had expired.

It was only from the new millennium, with most Nazi war criminals dead, that Germany's courts began to cautiously address the sins of the past. Even then, trials such as that of the alleged Nazi death camp guard John Demjanjuk in 2011 were rare. The 2015 conviction against Oskar Groening, the so-called 'Bookkeeper of Auschwitz', only took place after Groening himself came forward in protest at the rise of Holocaust denial in Germany.

Wrong place, wrong time

As the old generation passed a new generation of Neo-Nazis took its place, and the deep state switched from protecting former fascists to covering for the activities of actively operating extreme right-wing groups with whom they sympathized or whose help they needed.

This came to light in 2013, during the trial of Beate Zschäpe, the surviving member of a terrorist organization called the National Socialist Underground (NSU) that had waged a 13-year murder campaign against immigrants in Germany that left eight Turks, one Greek-German locksmith and a German policewoman dead. One of the prosecution witnesses was Andreas Temme, who in 2006 had been a customer in a Kassel internet café when its owner, Halit Yozgat, a 21-year-old man of Turkish descent, was shot dead by NSU members Uwe Mundlos and Uwe Böhnhardt. Temme testified that he had neither seen nor heard anything, but what really surprised the court was the revelation that he was an intelligence operative investigating far-right underground groups. Cross-examined on this, and asked why he had not come forward at the time of the murder, Temme claimed his presence in the internet café had been entirely coincidental. He had not spoken to the murder investigators, he said, because he was embarrassed: he did not want his heavily pregnant wife to find out he had been using the café to visit internet dating sites.

When the press looked into Temme's background they found he had known right-wing sympathies and, in his youth, had been nicknamed 'little Adolf' because of his outspoken views. Digging deeper to see if Temme was a rogue agent or part of a wider intelligence agency action, they were blocked by the state interior ministry. A public outcry erupted over what looked like a cover-up and an official investigation was launched. Although the investigation report was completed in 2014, the interior ministry of justice declared it could not be released in full and uncensored form until 2134 (though this date was later reduced to 2054).

With a network of underground Neo-Nazi sources and paid informants to safeguard, not to mention undercover agents to conceal, the intelligence service's reluctance to be more open about its activities is understandable. But when secret agents witness or even participate in racially motivated hate crimes it calls into question what those intelligence services are trying to achieve, and whether deep state elements have an interest in fomenting racial disharmony.

The new Neo-Nazis

This blurred line between covert infiltration and complicity was crossed in the summer of 2019, when a group of Neo-Nazis calling themselves Nordkreuz ('Northern Cross') was found to have compiled a 'death list' of left-wing and liberal targets whose details they had accessed via classified police records. At least one of the 30-strong group was part of a special police 'strike' team and the cell was found to have links with other officers and security service agents.

The Nordkreuz revelations came weeks after a far-right activist called Stephan Ernst confessed to the murder of the pro-

Members of Germany's elite Kommando Spezialkräfte unit. A large number of its members had associations with the far right, and have been linked to a variety of plots to assassinate political opponents on the left.

immigration politician Walter Lübcke, prompting accusations that Germany's intelligence services were, at best, turning a blind eye to right-wing extremism. This may have been why, in September 2019, Germany's military intelligence chiefs ordered an inquiry into the elite KSK (Kommando Spezialkräfte) counter-terrorism unit. Far-right affiliations within the 1,000-man force were found to be 'extraordinarily high' and dated back to at least the 1990s, when the KSK began holding an annual party to celebrate Adolf Hitler's birthday.

This comes at a time when far-right parties such as the NPD (Nationaldemokratische Partei Deutschlands, or National Democratic Party) and AfD (Alternative für Deutschland, or Alternative for Germany) are on the rise, a 'legitimate' corollary to the deep state seditionaries whose interests they share and whose actions have been facilitated by an intelligence service with a law-and-order and nationalist agenda. While there is not yet a formally organized deep state of Neo-Nazis, far-right politicians and government security services, their shared desire for a strong, secure and 'pure' Germany has disturbing echoes of a recent history few outside their cabal want to see revisited.

THE UNITED KINGDOM

Class matters in the United Kingdom – not just social class but the class you sit in at school, though of course the two are often linked. For at least two centuries, a privileged elite has had a disproportionately large influence on British politics, finance, security, the higher civil service, the media, the military and business. It's an old-boy network centred around the public school-to-Oxbridge 'pipeline' that for generations has provided the country's leaders. It's a network that, come what may, looks after its own.

In this study of the UK's elitist deep state we'll examine in particular how its needs and wants affect the way the country is run politically and administratively, and how the vested interests it represents in the worlds of business and, increasingly, finance, affect the nation's destiny – especially regarding Brexit, the great national issue of recent times.

The cream of the crop?

The facts about the UK's old-boy network, as we'll call this deep state, speak for themselves. Since 1900, 71 per cent of British prime ministers have attended the universities of Oxford or Cambridge. It's 77 per cent since Great Britain's first-ever PM, Robert Walpole (1721–42), from King's College, Cambridge. In that same period since Walpole's time, just 1 per cent of the population gained an Oxbridge degree. This is as it should be, perhaps, as Oxbridge is unashamedly elitist. But the best people it accepts are supposed to be the intellectual elite, which most of them are, rather than the richest, the most privileged or the best connected, though that is also undoubtedly the case, too. Just 7 per cent of the UK population are wealthy enough to attend public schools, but their students take up around 45 per cent of Oxbridge places.

More than 50 per cent of UK-educated names on the *Sunday Times* Rich List went to public school, as did 45 per cent of Conservative Party MPs (it's 15 per cent for the Labour Party) and 53 per cent of the last cabinet of Theresa May (St Hugh's College, Oxford) in 2019. Seventy-one per cent of senior UK judges are Oxbridge alumni, while 60 per cent of civil service permanent secretaries and 57 per cent of members of the House of Lords are privately educated. It's a situation similar to that in France, with its *grandes écoles* system, or America's Ivy League.

On the whole, the privileged few exercise their power benevolently, if not fairly, favouring a broadly paternalistic approach to public life. This goes some way to explaining what some saw as the establishment's wrong-headed response to the Brexit referendum result of 2016, where it was accused of seeking to overturn the will of the people on the assumption that voters

Oxford University is alma mater to just over half of the United Kingdom's prime ministers.

had not properly understood the complicated issues involved. Ironically, one of the biggest beneficiaries of the backlash against supposed deep-state establishment 'remoaners' was Boris Johnson (Eton; Balliol College, Oxford), one of the über-elite, who coasted to an 80-seat majority in the 2019 general election with a promise to 'get Brexit done'.

The coup that never was

Although the old-boy deep state operates benignly for the most part, in 1968 a section of it went on the offensive against what it saw as a threat to both national security and its own privileged position.

It is fair to say that Britain's establishment has always been wary of socialism. Left-wing politics, for most of this class, is something to be dabbled with at university and then abandoned as youthful folly thereafter. The consequences of not doing this result in unfortunate and embarrassing examples such as Kim Philby (Westminster School; Trinity College, Cambridge) and Guy Burgess (Eton; Trinity College, Cambridge), who took things further and spied for the Soviet Union through the 1930s, '40s and '50s, remaining undetected for so long because of their elite deep-state backgrounds.

When Labour's Harold Wilson (Jesus College, Oxford) became prime minister in 1964 a shiver ran through the deep state. Although a brilliant scholar, becoming one of Britain's youngest-ever dons at just 21 years old, Wilson was also a grammar-school boy; not quite the right sort, according to some of his more privileged contemporaries. When Wilson once recounted in parliament how as a child in the 1930s he had been so poor that he had no shoes to wear, the thoroughbred Tory leader Harold Macmillan (Eton; Balliol College, Oxford), in a remark that perfectly captured the era's 'know your place' culture, retorted that, 'if Mr Wilson did not have boots to go to school, it was because he was too big for them'.

Someone else who believed that Wilson was too big for his boots was Cecil Harmsworth King (Winchester College; Christ Church, Oxford), a press baron whose stable of titles included the *Daily Mirror*, then the world's largest-selling daily newspaper with a largely working-class readership – the 'little man', as King referred to his typical reader. In King's mind, he and his newspaper had delivered Wilson's electoral victory and he wanted acknowledgement and reward for doing so. But when Harold Wilson duly offered King a peerage he was rebuffed. King wanted an earldom, which Wilson was not prepared to grant. From that moment King became Harold Wilson's most implacable enemy, using the *Daily Mirror* to attack the Labour government relentlessly and decrying the party's failure to manage the economy. For a brief while, King became involved in discussions with Lord Cromer (Eton; Trinity College, Cambridge), the governor of the Bank of England, with a view to deposing Harold Wilson and replacing him with someone regarded as more attuned to the nation's – and the establishment's – needs.

When Cromer left the Bank in 1966, King carried on plotting. He first attempted to recruit fellow newspapermen to his scheme.

The *Daily Mirror* editor Hugh Cudlipp (left school at 14) was amenable, while the *Daily Telegraph*'s Bill Deedes (Harrow) and William Rees-Mogg (Charterhouse; Balliol College, Oxford) of *The Times* were ambivalent. Openly hostile was the technology minister, Tony Benn (Westminster School; New College, Oxford), who told Wilson that something was afoot after King approached him. Forewarned, Wilson made plans to defend himself against any attempted putsch, while King's City of London co-conspirators, possibly alarmed at what a King–Wilson power struggle would mean for the economy, quietly withdrew from the plot. But even though the prime minister was fully aware of King's plans, and despite the fact that many of his coup backers had now deserted him, the embittered press baron ploughed on regardless.

On 8 May 1968, Cecil King invited Lord Louis Mountbatten (Royal Naval College) to dinner and asked him if he would lead an emergency government following a coup against Wilson. A shocked Mountbatten made his excuses and left. Two days later, King published an incendiary front-page attack on Wilson in the *Daily Mirror* under the heading 'ENOUGH IS ENOUGH'. In it, King claimed that the country was headed for ruin under an economically incompetent Labour government and that Wilson had to go. King hoped his article would inspire revolutionary fervour in his army of *Daily Mirror* readers. It didn't. Three weeks later, King's board of directors ousted him in a coup of their own and Wilson remained as prime minister until 1970, and again from 1974–76.

The full extent of King's plot remains unclear. In his 1987 memoir *Spycatcher*, which the UK government tried to ban, the former MI5 operative Peter Wright (St Peter's College, Oxford) claimed his agency had been involved in the plot and that King had been 'a longtime agent'. Wright also alleged that a right-wing contingent within MI5 had bugged and surveilled Wilson, whom they suspected of being a Soviet spy. This was a subject in which Britain's intelligence services were well-versed, as their ranks had

An unlikely revolutionary: Daily Mirror *owner Cecil Harmsworth King formed a deep state cabal to bring down prime minister Harold Wilson.*

formerly included Russian agents such as the 'Cambridge Five' of Kim Philby, Guy Burgess, Donald Maclean, Sir Anthony Blunt and John Cairncross (all Trinity College, Cambridge), and the Soviet double-agent George Blake (Downham College, Cambridge).

Peter Wright's revelations about off-the-books secret service actions were nothing new, however. Throughout the 1950s, for example, MI6 maintained its own slush fund independent of any government control. The account was held at Holt's Military Bank at 22 Whitehall and contained up to £1.4 million (£39 million/ US$50.5 million in today's money), most of which was destined for unauthorized operations in the Middle East with codenames such as Scant, Scream, Straggle and Sawdust, the last of which was thought to be a plan to destabilize President Nasser in Egypt. To this day, the origin of the money at Holt's is unknown: when the Treasury found out about the account in 1952, MI6's 'C', Sir Stewart Menzies (Eton; Grenadier Guards), would only say that the funds came from 'well-wishers . . . including a particularly large sum from an American'.

Who really runs Britain?

In 1980, a new sitcom on BBC TV focused on the inner workings of the old-boy deep state in Whitehall's corridors of power. *Yes Minister*, and its successor *Yes Prime Minister*, which ran until 1988, followed the career of hapless politician Jim Hacker, who at every turn is thwarted and outwitted by his civil service permanent secretary, Sir Humphrey Appleby. The show was so accurate in portraying how civil service elites follow their own agendas, often against government instruction, that ever after Whitehall mandarins have been known colloquially as 'Sir Humphreys'. They are the embodiment of the never-changing elite deep state against here-today-gone-tomorrow politicians, the type of men (it's almost always men) who run things from the comfortable leather armchairs of exclusive gentlemen's clubs in St James's, where state policy is made and unmade with the proverbial 'quiet word' over aged whisky.

Yes Minister was first broadcast just months after the 1979 electoral victory of Margaret Thatcher (Somerville College, Oxford). Thatcher and the old-boy deep state were at odds from day one. Like Harold Wilson, Thatcher was an upstart – a grocer's daughter. To traditional Tories, she was 'TBW', that bloody woman. But the new prime minister did not care. Her mission, as she saw it, was to overhaul Britain's 'nanny state', making the country more competitive and efficient through the imposition of a free-market economic model that ran counter to the one-nation conservatism that had until then dominated both her party and the old-boy network that ran the country.

Yet while Margaret Thatcher was absolutely one of British history's great disruptors and undeniably changed the country forever, the old-boy deep state went into only temporary retreat during her 10-year reign. By the new millennium it was back, stronger than ever. In 2005, for example, senior civil servants at the Department for Education and Skills blocked and then watered down proposals by the Labour government of Tony Blair (Fettes; St John's College, Oxford) to give parents greater choice over which schools their children went to. A few years later, in 2011, the civil service body the Major Projects Authority (MPA) prepared a study that was so critical of the contentious HS2 rail scheme that the government refused to publish it – although, of course, the report was leaked anyway and helped to further undermine what, for the administrative deep state, is an expensive and messy drain on public resources they would rather see shelved.

By 2012, Prime Minister David Cameron (Eton; Brasenose College, Oxford) was publicly complaining that senior civil servants were blocking government initiatives they disagreed with, particularly one aimed at reducing the power of civil service experts and increasing the influence of politically appointed special advisors. In a line that could have come straight from an episode of *Yes Minister*, the nation's top civil servant Sir Jeremy Heywood (Hertford College, Oxford) told a House of Commons committee that, 'Part of our role is to give advice, as to whether something will work, whether something is contrary to the law. Occasionally that will come across as trying to slow things down or stop things happening – that is part of our job.' Shortly after, Cameron's civil service plans were quietly shelved.

A divisive Brexit

Needless to say, the establishment elite was accused of interfering in the biggest issue of recent times: Brexit. It was an event that did not just divide the nation; it split the deep state too.

Britain joined what was then called the European Community (EC) in 1973 and, on 5 June 1975, the nation's membership was confirmed in a referendum by a margin of 67–33 per cent. This came as a tremendous relief to the UK's security services, which wanted Britain to join what was a strong mainland European alliance against the Soviet Union. To this end, MI6 and senior figures at the Foreign Office set up and funded several pro-EC organizations to influence public opinion, notably the European League for Economic Co-operation (ELEC), fronted by the businessman and politician Alistair McAlpine (born in the Dorchester Hotel; Stowe School). So secret was ELEC's deep-state backing, which may also have included CIA cash, that McAlpine himself initially did not know about it.

Forty years later, the deep state was at it again – allegedly. This time it was Whitehall civil servants, Remain-supporting politicians from across the political spectrum and the BBC that were accused of trying to reverse the Leave result of 52–48 per cent that was delivered on 23 June 2016. The Electoral Commission, for example, was accused of censuring campaign spending violations by Brexit advocates such as Matthew Elliott (London School of Economics) and Dominic Cummings (Exeter College, Oxford) of the Vote Leave campaign, and Darren Grimes (University of Brighton) of the youth group BeLeave, while ignoring over-spending by the Remain movement. It was alleged that both sides lied and spread disinformation throughout the campaign. The BBC was a Remain mouthpiece, Leave supporters maintained; newspapers such as the *Sun*, the *Daily Telegraph*, the *Daily Express* and the *Daily Mail* printed unverified Leave-supplied lies, Remainers complained. Whether these accusations were true or not, they echoed a long-standing tradition of British press owners pushing their agendas through their titles, from Cecil King's 'Enough is enough' *Daily Mirror* vendetta to the Australian-American Rupert Murdoch's 'It's the *Sun* wot won it' headline after the Tory party's general election victory in 1992 openly celebrated that newspaper's influence.

Allegations of Russian interference in the Brexit campaign were also made by the pro-EU camp (see p.233). At the time of writing, an official report into possible Russian meddling has yet to be made public. Its publication was delayed for unexplained reasons until after the 2019 general election, which was won on a 'Get Brexit Done' platform by a Conservative Party whose campaign funding was augmented to the tune of several million pounds by wealthy Russian donors.

Hedging their bets

When Boris Johnson's Conservative government passed the Brexit withdrawal agreement bill in January 2020, marking the beginning of Britain's departure from the EU, the attention of Remain supporters turned from asking *how* Britons were persuaded to vote to leave the EU to *why* they were encouraged to do so.

While 17,410,742 Leave voters were very happy when the referendum result came in, a select few were happier than others. Crispin Odey (Harrow; Christ Church, Oxford) is a hedge fund manager and Conservative Party donor. It has been claimed that his company, Odey Asset Management, made US$300 million on referendum night by 'betting' on a victory for Leave when most people's money was on Remain. Jacob Rees-Mogg (Eton; Trinity College, Oxford), the Tory MP and then-chairman of the pro-Brexit European Research Group (ERG), is an old acquaintance of Crispin Odey. In 2007 Odey helped Rees-Mogg set up Somerset Capital Management (SCM), an investment fund in which Rees-Mogg retains a 15 per cent share. According to a 2019 report in the UK Channel 4 documentary programme *Dispatches*, SCM's Brexit-related profits since 2016 are £47 million, with Rees-Mogg's share estimated at £7 million, a figure he refutes. Finally, Nigel Farage (Dulwich College), the man who more than any other made Brexit happen, has been accused of profiting from the referendum result too, by placing currency bets on a successful Leave result.

While speculating on the outcome of political voting is not illegal, it is unlawful to do it while in receipt of inside information. Farage's supposed Brexit windfall was said to have been based on his receiving embargoed exit poll information on the night of the referendum in advance of the official 10.00pm release date, allowing him to falsely speculate twice on live television that he thought the Leave campaign had lost. This helped to shorten the odds on a Remain victory, and lengthen those on a Leave win. Farage denies these speculations, but allegations of insider trading continue to dog the financiers and fund managers who made a killing from the Brexit result.

With the Leave vote secured, at least one hedge fund capitalized on the victory in a perhaps surprising way, when SCM set up a fund in Dublin, safely within the Eurozone that Jacob Rees-Mogg, SCM's founder and large shareholder, had campaigned so vigorously to leave. SCM's Irish expansion is all the more perplexing as the hedge funds' main reason for supporting Brexit was to avoid EU regulations such as the Alternative Investment Fund Managers Directive (AIFMD) and the Markets in Financial Instruments Directive II (Mifid II) that introduced taxes and restrictions on investment transactions. 'I think there are real risks – long-term structural risks – to remaining in the EU, which we are now free from,' said Rees-Mogg after the referendum result. He also maintains that, as a serving MP, he is not involved in any of SCM's business or investment decisions.

Pay to play

The close association of the Leave campaign and hedge fund support is one that grew as traditional business backing for Brexit waned. When the Confederation of British Industry (CBI) came out for Remain in 2016 not everyone in the Leave campaign was dismayed. 'Fuck business,' Boris Johnson later declared – safe in the knowledge that his camp was being generously backed by the finance industry, and that this support would carry over to the Conservative Party once it unequivocally committed itself to extracting the UK from the EU quickly.

This changing of the guard from business to finance can be tracked clearly in the composition of the Leader's Group lobbying association, set up in 2003 and open only to donors who contribute £50,000 or more to the Conservative Party. Until around 2010 it was dominated by traditional business, such as manufacturers and retailers. Today, hedge funds, private banking and private equity account for 40 per cent of Leader's Group contributions, amounting to £50 million since 2010. That cash – at least £13 million for the 2019 election campaign – buys its donors many things, including direct access to the party leadership. In September 2019 the former Conservative chancellor of the exchequer Philip Hammond (University College, Oxford) wrote in *The Times* that '[Boris] Johnson is backed by speculators who have bet billions on a hard Brexit – and there is only one option that works for them: a crash-out no-deal that sends the currency tumbling and inflation soaring'.

If Hammond's comments are correct, it means that a handful of financial gamblers hold Britain's economic and political fate in their hands. Its rival administrative deep state and the courts stand in their way at present, which is why concerns were raised in early 2020 when the hedge fund-financed Conservative government floated plans to 'merge-and-purge' civil service departments and make Whitehall's bureaucrats sit annual exams. This came on top of a promise by Boris Johnson to reform the justice system after the Supreme Court ruled his September 2019 prorogation of Parliament was unlawful.

With rival deep states going head-to-head in post-Brexit Britain, the 2020s promise to be an interesting decade.

CHAPTER 3

THE MIDDLE EAST

RELIGIOUS STRIFE, OIL and disputed borders – each of these elements on their own guarantee regional strife, but the Middle East has a surfeit of all three and is consequently the most volatile area on Earth. And where there is volatility there are deep states. Here we'll look at four countries – and five, possibly six, deep states – that best illustrate the issues affecting this unsettled area. Israel and Turkey have their problems with religious deep states, while the latter nation has battled with a secular, establishment deep state, too. In Egypt we'll see just how ruthless and devious a military deep state can be, while the example of Iran shows how a nation can successfully manufacture and export deep state networks in order to subvert the power of neighbours and rivals.

ISRAEL

The largest of the many questions facing modern Israel is what to do with the millions of Palestinians who live within its borders –

and where those borders are. Many Israelis support the 'two-state' approach, with the self-governing territories of Gaza and the West Bank serving as homelands for Palestinians. Opposing this are those who believe Israel is one and indivisible, the Promised Land given to them by God.

In recent years this issue has destroyed the old left-wing Labour Party/right-wing Likud Party consensus and realigned traditional lines of support. Today, Israeli political life consists of a centre ground facing off against a right-wing split into secular-nationalist and ultra-Orthodox religious factions, with each, according to the other, dominated by deep-state interests. The person at the centre of this factionalism is the most successful – and therefore contentious – Israeli politician of recent times. Depending on your political affiliation, six-times Likud prime minister Benjamin Netanyahu is either a corrupt operator whose journey ever-rightward in search of votes has made him the captive of an ultra-Orthodox deep state, or he's 'Mr Security', an implacable protector of Israel being persecuted by a left-wing conspiracy.

The influence of the Haredis

As leader of a right-wing party, Netanyahu naturally took a firm line on Arab-related issues by cracking down on Palestinian protests and curbing the rights of Palestinians to move more freely, or at all, between Gaza and the West Bank and Israel. But Netanyahu went far beyond this. He allowed Israeli settlers from the ultra-Orthodox Haredi community to move into Palestinian-designated land in the West Bank, which led to protests and, inevitably, deaths. The two largest Israeli settlements in the West Bank are both Haredi, and Haredis make up 30 per cent of all West Bank settlers. In September 2019 Netanyahu announced plans to annex the Jordan Valley – an area representing around 22 per cent of the West Bank. This was condemned as a breach of international law, an attack on Palestinian rights – and a shameless pitch for Haredi votes.

Even for a critic of the two-state plan such as Netanyahu, this was provocative. Concerned Likud voters began to desert Netanyahu in favour of less religiously compromised right-wingers such as Avigdor Lieberman, whose Yisrael Beiteinu Party helped to deny Likud outright victories in general elections in April and September 2019. By the end of 2019, Netanyahu was cornered. His

Critics argue prime minister Benjamin Netanyahu is jeopardizing his country's future by courting support among Israel's hard-line orthodox Jews.

pursuit of Haredi votes had pushed him to the right, at precisely the same time that the Haredi community was moving even further to the right itself. Where the Haredi had once been composed mostly of Ashkenazi Jews of European origin, who tended to be more 'liberal' in their ultra-Orthodoxy and who supported the United Torah Judaism Party, by the late 2010s the movement was made up of a higher proportion of Sephardic Jews of Middle Eastern origin, represented by the Shas Party. Shas-supporting Haredis are uncompromising in their beliefs and will not tolerate the idea of two-statism. As well as a feeling of otherness towards Gentiles, many Haredi do not even accept secular Jews as their compatriots – and with Netanyahu so dependent on them they can relentlessly push their theological agenda, whatever the implications for the people and the politics of Israel.

An uneasy settlement

The most vocal criticism of Benjamin Netanyahu and his ultra-Orthodox deep-state handlers came from the Israeli military and secret services, leading to allegations that they themselves comprised a deep state dedicated to destroying the prime minister.

As Netanyahu moved further to the right, undermining the fragile two-state consensus in the process, the centre ground of Israeli politics coalesced around a new organization, the Blue and White Party. It was formed in early 2019 by Benny Gantz, the ex-head of Israel's armed forces, and boasts a large number of serving and retired generals among its supporters, many of whom are among the 300 high-ranking former army, police and intelligence officers who have also joined an organization called Commanders for Israel's Security, a pressure group dedicated to promoting the two-state solution.

For Gantz and other centrists (which is to say centrists compared to Netanyahu) only the two-state solution can ensure Israel's survival. The biggest existential threat to the country is not traditional enemies such as Saudi Arabia, Syria and Egypt, they say, it's demographics. Broadly speaking, there are 6.6 million Jews in Israel and 2 million Palestinians. There are also 5 million Palestinians in Gaza and the West Bank. Incorporate these territories back into Israel and the Jewish people will immediately become a minority in their own country. Add to that the civil strife, war and terrorism that would inevitably follow the abolition of the West Bank and Gaza and it's easy to see why the generals are worried.

Benjamin Netanyahu became prime minister for the second time in 2009, and for the next 10 years he systematically ground down public support for the two-state consensus, from almost 70 per cent to less than 50 per cent – amongst both Jews and Palestinians. He has admittedly been helped in this by Palestinian terrorist attacks on Israel, as well as by Palestinian leaders in Gaza refusing to accept the existence of Israel as a state. With public belief in the two-state settlement in decline, centrists feel that time is running out to save Israel. The answer, they believe, is to destroy Netanyahu – at the ballot box and beyond.

An uneasy balance

Netanyahu will not give up without a fight, of course – not an entirely legal one, it's claimed. In the April 2019 general election, the first of two that year, Netanyahu-supporting activists planted some 1,200 hidden cameras inside polling stations in Arab communities. This was done in direct contravention of Israeli electoral rules and was undertaken specifically to monitor which parties Arab-Israelis were voting for. While Netanyahu shrugged off the story when it came to light, citing concerns of possible electoral fraud as a reason for the cameras, it was an embarrassing revelation. In the end, Netanyahu's Likud and Benny Gantz's Blue and White Party both won 35 seats, meaning that neither secured a parliamentary majority. When coalition talks broke down, Netanyahu, as the incumbent, got to stay on as prime minister as head of a minority government.

In the September 2019 election Likud did slightly worse, securing 32 seats. Although the Blue and White Party won 33 seats, Netanyahu again held on to the prime ministership after coalition negotiations failed. This slight shift away from Likud may be indicative of changes among Israeli voters who want to distance themselves from Netanyahu's increasingly uncompromising stance. But it should also be considered that the election took place with Netanyahu facing corruption charges for trying to buy favourable media coverage and for receiving cash and gifts in return for political favours. This too could have affected his support, and if the cases against Netanyahu are dismissed at any point some of his voters may well return to the fold.

Netanyahu claimed that the corruption allegations were part of a centrist deep-state plot to discredit him and even labelled it an attempted coup involving the judiciary and the police. His own supporters certainly believed him, as in December 2019 Netanyahu was re-elected as leader of Likud by 72 per cent of the party membership. In January 2020 he also tried to persuade the Israeli parliament to postpone his corruption trial until after the March 2020 election, knowing that if he retained the prime ministership he would be immune from prosecution for his term of office – an incentive, if ever there was one, to hold on to power at all costs. As it turned out, the spring 2020 general election was just as inconclusive as those in 2019. Likud emerged from the poll with 36 seats and Blue and White stayed steady on 33 seats, resulting in a deal between Benjamin Netanyahu and Benny Gantz for their two parties to form a government of national unity – with 'Bibi' as prime minister, naturally.

By pushing Israel's politics to the outer limits, Netanyahu has unleashed powerful and opposing religious, ethnic and military deep-state forces that he and anyone else will struggle to control. Israel's centrists repeatedly point out that Netanyahu is only thinking about the short term, about winning whatever election is in front of him or ensuring he stays out of prison, and that with every renewal of his prime ministership the end of Israel moves one step closer.

IRAN

Iran's history goes back at least 2,500 years, and it's rarely been harmonious. Known as Persia until the middle of the 20th century, it was a regional superpower from classical antiquity to the late Middle Ages. It's a status it is attempting to regain today.

Deep states have played their part in Iran's history, particularly in the last century or so. In that time the country has gone from suffering at the hands of a deep state to masterminding its own network of deep-state enterprises across the Middle East.

The British connection

In the 19th century, Britain kept an eye on Persia, which was a strategically important territory bordering both India (the part that is Pakistan today), the jewel in the crown of the empire, and Afghanistan, where British and Russian imperialists skirmished for control in what was euphemistically known as the 'Great Game'.

When oil was discovered in Persia in May 1908, Britain's interest sharpened. English entrepreneur William Knox D'Arcy was the lucky man who struck black gold, and he was shrewd enough to sign a deal with Persia that exploited the ruling Qajar royal family's lack of business acumen. In return for exclusive drilling rights, D'Arcy would pay Persia just 16 per cent of his self-declared net profits and exempt himself from tax and customs payments. He called his business the Anglo-Persian Oil Company (APOC) and, in 1914, sold a controlling stake in it to the British government. For the next 65 years APOC was a constant, if not always welcome, presence in Persian life. When the Bakhtiari people of western Persia objected to APOC drilling in their ancestral homelands their leaders were bought off with company shares, while the Arab tribal chief Shaikh Kaz'al was bribed to allow APOC access to the Persian Gulf. These and other deals were made behind the backs of Persia's rulers.

When the Qajar royal family realized it had been fleeced by Knox, it lobbied APOC to rebalance their arrangement. This irked APOC at first, but as the Persians increased pressure the company's patience snapped and in 1921 the Qajar regime was removed in a military coup. There is some debate as to the level of APOC and the British government's complicity in the regime change but, not uncoincidentally, by the mid-1920s APOC had renegotiated its contract with Persia's new rulers on even more favourable terms than before, most notably a 60-year drilling rights extension and a concession by the country to waive its right to annul the agreement.

Breaking away

This is not to say that Iran, as the country was renamed in 1935, fully accepted APOC's deep state dominion. Far from it. Iran, for example, courted US oil companies in an effort to offset APOC's monopoly and supported the Axis powers in World War II. But these acts of rebellion only brought further trouble. The crisis point came in the early 1950s, when the nationalist prime minister Mohammad Mosaddegh came to power. In opposition to his nominal boss, the Shah of Iran, Mosaddegh introduced a parliamentary bill to nationalize the country's oil industry. An alarmed APOC used its British government connections to approach the CIA and asked it to unseat the rabble-rousing and, APOC claimed, Soviet Union-supporting Mosaddegh. This it duly did, in August 1953, helping to organize a seizure of power by the Persian general Fazlollah Zahedi in an operation known as Codename Ajax. Interestingly, this was the first time the CIA had successfully planned and executed a *coup d'état* and they took this experience into the regime change they effected in Guatemala the following year (see pp.145–51).

Following the coup, the Shah, who had been driven into exile by Mosaddegh, returned to power and became an increasingly repressive ruler, coming down particularly hard on the growing Islamic fundamentalist movement in his country. One of the religious leaders he drove into exile was the cleric Ayatollah Ruhollah Khomeini, who in 1979 was to return to Iran at the head of a revolutionary movement that deposed the Shah and declared the country an Islamic Republic. APOC, which rebranded as British Petroleum, or BP, in 1982, cut its losses in Iran and turned its deep state attentions elsewhere. The Iranian well had run dry.

EXPORTING TERROR

After 1979, Iran's religious leaders applied their experiences from APOC, British government and CIA deep state interference to their own foreign policy operations. Iran today is one of the Middle East's main 'exporters' of deep state infiltration, to both its enemies and allies. This is partly motivated by a desire to manage the regional influence of the USA – 'the Great Satan', in Ayatollah Khomeini's phrase – and other non-Muslim states such as Russia (a sometime ally) and the UK. But Iran's sponsoring of destabilizing

Iran's government nationalized its oil industry in 1951 – and was ousted in a UK- and US-led coup two years later as a result.

influences is also an outgrowth of its campaign to control the Muslim world – or at least the part that shares its particular beliefs.

Like Christianity, Islam is not a monolithic religion. Its equivalent of the factionalism between Catholics and Protestants is the split between Sunni and Shia Muslims. Iran is the largest Shia-majority nation, followed by Iraq. All other Islamic nations are Sunni-dominated, with Egypt, Saudi Arabia and Pakistan the major players. Iran sees itself as the protector of Shia Islam, which is traditionally radical and expansionist, while Saudi Arabia is the self-appointed guardian of more conservative Sunni interests. Up to 90 per cent of Muslims are Sunni, so Shias have always seen themselves as a persecuted but righteous minority.

The high-profile killing of the Iranian military leader Qassem Soleimani in January 2020 by a targeted US drone strike exposed the full extent of Iran's 'Axis of Resistance' across the Middle East. Since 1998, Soleimani had been the head of Iran's special-ops Quds Force and over 22 years he had created a huge network of military and political deep state supporters, fighters, agents and insurgents working to further Shia – and Iranian – interests.

The list of Soleimani's achievements is remarkable. For example, he transformed Iraq from Iran's would-be destroyer into an acquiescent client state by infiltrating the country with pro-Iran militias and politicians following the 2003 removal from power of Saddam Hussein by US-led forces. By the time government was restored to Iraq in 2005, Soleimani's proxies were in the ascendancy. Jalal Talibani, Iraqi's president in 2005–14, was firmly in Soleimani's pocket, as have been all post-2005 prime ministers. Around 150,000 Iran-affiliated militia, known as Popular Mobilization Forces (PMF) are embedded in Iraq and have formed a political grouping called the Fatah Alliance. So confident was Soleimani of his deep-state dominance of Iraq and elsewhere that, in 2008, he boasted in a message to the US military command in Iraq how 'I, Qassem Soleimani, control Iran's policy for Iraq, Syria, Lebanon, Gaza, and Afghanistan.'

Iran's international terrorism mastermind Qassem Soleimani, assassinated by a US air strike in January 2020.

Friends in high places

With Iraq under control, Soleimani directed his attention to Sunni-dominated Syria when civil war erupted there in 2011. Its beleaguered president, Bashar al-Assad, was neither a Sunni nor a Shia but a member of a small Muslim splinter sect known as the Alawites. With rebel forces, Kurds and the jihadists of Islamic State and al-Qaeda (both Sunni) ranged against him, Assad was only too pleased to welcome the Shia-aligned Hezbollah fighters ordered into Syria by Soleimani. These battle-hardened veterans quickly made impressive gains against Assad's enemies and, in the process, occupied Syria's Golan Heights. This gave Iran a deep-state foothold in Syria, and provided Hezbollah with a strategic position from which to launch attacks on its sworn enemy, Israel.

Hezbollah is a long-standing client of Iran, which finances it to the tune of around US$700 million annually. Headquartered in the Bekaa Valley of southern Lebanon, Hezbollah has evolved from a narrowly focused anti-Israeli terror group into a private army and political party. It returns MPs to Lebanon's parliament and holds seats in the cabinet, which gives it the power of veto over government policy. In virtually every major political decision it makes, Hezbollah follows Iran's lead. In infiltrating Iraq, Lebanon and Syria to its west, Iran established a deep-state arc of influence across the Middle East that the late King Hussein of Jordan called a 'Shiite crescent'.

To its east, Iran has also made incursions into Pakistan, which contains a significant Shia minority of about 35 million followers, by supporting anti-Taliban fighters along the country's border with Afghanistan (the Taliban being an extremist Sunni sect that sees Shias as infidels worthy only of death). Further south, Soleimani and Iran played a clever but deadly game in Yemen, an unstable and troubled Sunni nation whose large Shia minority is in revolt against its rulers. By supporting the Shia rebels with arms and cash,

Iran ensured that its regional rival Saudi Arabia, which borders Yemen, was dragged into the distracting, expensive and draining conflict.

A master manipulator and political-religious extremist such as Soleimani was always going to be a prize trophy for the Americans, and his death left a massive power vacuum in the Middle East. But if this leads to the collapse of the elaborate deep state edifice he constructed it's not clear if what will emerge from the ruins will be better or worse than what went before.

EGYPT

The military has never been far from power in modern Egypt. From 1952 until the 'Arab Spring' revolution of early 2011, the country was ruled by military or military-backed governments, all led by serving or former armed forces men. The popular uprising of 2011 was supposed to change all that, with its call for 'bread, freedom and social justice' and an end to president Hosni Mubarak's corrupt and repressive regime. However, Egypt's story since the 2011 protests is a vivid example of how those hopes were not only defeated but used by the military deep state to ultimately strengthen its hold on power.

Military manoeuvres

The former air force officer Hosni Mubarak became Egypt's president in 1981, following the assassination of his predecessor Anwar Sadat by Islamic fundamentalists. For the next 30 years he ruled the country with two guiding principles: that Egypt's military maintain its dominant position at all costs; and that religious fundamentalism be kept as far from politics as possible.

Mubarak's time in office has been described as a kleptocracy, where the president, his family and a cabal of high-ranking military officers helped themselves to billions of dollars of state funds. On the everyday level there was the endemic favour-trading, cronyism and a form of clientelism Egyptians call *wasta*, or 'who you know'. In all cases, the armed forces were at the head of the queue when there was state money to be had. Alongside its role as defender of national security, Egypt's military also operates as a highly profitable business. Military-run enterprises such as the National Services Products Organization and the Armed Forces Engineering Authority generate vast revenues from their interests in infrastructure projects, farming, chemicals, mining, aviation and much else. All military business is conducted with little or no oversight or accountability.

The enrichment of Egypt's military elite meant the impoverishment of the people. Between 1999 and 2010, GDP grew at an annual average rate of 5 per cent, but in the same period the number of people living below the poverty line rose from 11 million to 21 million – almost a quarter of the population. So, when popular protests demanding democracy and freedom broke out across North Africa in late 2010 it was no surprise that the 'Arab Spring' spread to Egypt too.

The Arab Spring effect

If Mubarak thought his former military colleagues would protect him, he was wrong. The protests were so violent and passionate that the military deep state realized that only regime change would satisfy the rebels. When it was made clear that Egypt's armed forces would not support him in office, the 82-year-old president reluctantly stepped down in February 2011. With Mubarak gone and the protesters' demands partially met, the military deep state was happy to allow events to play out, satisfied that its pre-eminent position was no longer under threat – for now.

The Arab Spring unleashed many hitherto repressed groups in Egyptian society, including democrats, pan-Arabists, monarchists and nationalists. By far the most vocal faction was the fundamentalist Muslim Brotherhood, whose passionately expressed religious certainties resonated with millions of Egyptians. In the first post-Mubarak presidential elections in

2012 the Muslim Brotherhood-backed candidate Mohamed Morsi won a tightly contested battle, securing just under 52 per cent of the vote.

The armed forces would ordinarily have balked at this result: the Muslim Brotherhood was a radical group and technically an illegal (but tolerated) organization dedicated to refounding Egypt as a faith-based state. But Morsi was quick to reassure the military he had no intention of meddling in its business, and he was true to his word – for a few months, at least. But when the Muslim Brotherhood tried to muscle in on a military-controlled and money-spinning project to redevelop the Suez Canal the deep state was roused to action. Fortunately, it did not have to wait long for a pretext to act. Less than a year into his presidential term Morsi was showing himself to be a repressive, partisan and incompetent leader and by mid-2013 the people had taken to the streets to resist his rule.

A coordinated media campaign to undermine Morsi was initiated by the military, which also encouraged its business associates to fund a range of disrupting opposition parties. Almost overnight, a youth-based movement called Tamarod ('rebellion') appeared and began taking part in mass protests against Morsi. But, despite its youthful composition, Tamarod was not the spontaneous manifestation of teenage angst. It was set up and funded by the 58-year-old billionaire businessman Naguib Sawiris and organized by the military-controlled Ministry of Interior and the security services.

An embattled Mohamed Morsi was deposed and arrested in a military coup on 3 July 2013. Hundreds, possibly thousands, of pro- and anti-Morsi demonstrators died in the aftermath of the takeover. The Muslim Brotherhood was outlawed, leading to a resurgence of fundamentalist terrorism in Egypt that continues to this day and the jailing of up to 40,000 Muslim Brotherhood supporters as well as hundreds of executions. Morsi himself died in prison in June 2019.

Armoured personnel carriers are deployed during the military coup against Mohamed Morsi's government.

The deep state fights back

Following this messy flirtation with democracy, the military deep state decided it needed to take back control. To this end it put forward Abdel Fattah al-Sisi, army general, ex-director of military intelligence and former minister of defence, as its candidate to succeed Morsi. It is instructive how in this instance the military engineered Sisi's victory as a 'soft' seizure of power, a technique that has since been adopted by other deep states, for example in Thailand in 2019 (see pp.104–10).

On polling day in 2014, Egyptians were given just two choices for president: Sisi and Hamdeen Sabahi of the left-wing Popular Current Party. Twelve candidates had run in the 2012 election won by Morsi, but, with the exception of Sabahi, they had all been 'persuaded' by the men in uniform not to stand this time around. The campaign itself saw Sisi lionized in the media while Sabahi was ignored. Anti-Sisi demonstrations were banned and thousands of left-wingers and Muslim Brotherhood activists were rounded up and jailed. When the votes were counted Sisi had secured 97 per cent of the ballot – a margin unheard-of outside all but the most corrupt South American banana republics and African dictatorships.

Armed with an overwhelming 'mandate', Sisi set about embedding the military even deeper into the state through new legislation. The anodyne-sounding Law Number 32, for example, removed all of its business activities from public, political and legal scrutiny. Also, the method of making government appointments was changed so that the minister of defence could henceforth only be a serving military officer and was to be chosen not by politicians but by the Supreme Council of the Armed Forces (SCAF). The armed forces also secured appointees to many other government posts, and by 2018 two-thirds of Egypt's 27 regional governors were ex-military men.

Vote for me!

For his re-election campaign in 2018, Sisi offered more of the same. Giant government infrastructure projects became the almost exclusive preserve of military agencies, most notably the ambitious, some would say Ozymandian, construction of an as-yet unnamed new city in the desert around 50 km (31 miles) east of Cairo intended as Egypt's new administrative capital (NEC). The brainchild of President Sisi, the NEC (dubbed 'Sisi-City' by its detractors) will on completion house six million people, be home to a large proportion of Egypt's civil service and feature tens of thousands of offices, several gleaming, air-conditioned malls, a green space twice the size of New York's Central Park and a theme park bigger than Disneyland. At 700 km^2 (270 miles^2) it will be as large as Singapore.

In short, the NEC represents an almost bottomless bucket of free money for the army-run organization overseeing its development. The trouble is that it cannot find enough investors to build the place, for which estimated costs have risen from around US$40

A view of Egypt's New Administrative Capital, a vastly expensive and ambitious project which remains unfinished in 2020.

billion to just under US$60 billion at the last count. The NEC was supposed to be up and running by early 2020, but that date came and went with just a small proportion of the site approaching anything like completion. The state-run company in charge of this potentially ruinous white elephant is the Administrative Capital for Urban Development (ACUD), which is 51 per cent owned by Egypt's military (the minority 49 per cent share is controlled by the country's housing ministry). ACUD originally secured an agreement from the United Arab Emirates-based Capital City Planners to fund and carry out most of the NEC's construction, but this deal fell through when the two parties could not agree how payments should be made – code, according to some Egypt-watchers, for a failure to agree a suitable level of 'reward' to ACUD for granting the contract. Next on the list of ACUD's suitors was the China State Construction Engineering Corporation (CSCEC), followed by the China Fortune Land Development Company (CFLD), then Dubai's DP world, all of whom have been involved in long negotiations with the military-run agency – and with each other – to take on what is one of the largest building and engineering projects of the century so far.

In terms of rival 2018 presidential candidates, as in 2014, Sisi's potential opponents fell away one by one. Ahmed Konsowa, an army colonel with pro-democracy views, was simply jailed for six years in 2017 after announcing his plans to run, while the lawyer and human rights activists Khaled Ali was downed by sexual harassment allegations. Another candidate, former prime minister Ahmed Shafiq, was smeared as a Turkish agent and Muslim Brotherhood proxy, and placed under house arrest. Finally, General Sami Anan, a liberal seen as Sisi's strongest opponent, was arrested on charges of running for office without permission from his army superiors three days after announcing his candidature. Detained for two years, Anan was only released in 2019 when the election was safely over.

With all of his potential opponents jailed, defamed, or publicly humiliated, Sisi was left with just one rival in the 2018 election: Moussa Mostafa Moussa, of the tiny El-Ghad Party. Predictably, Sisi romped home with 96 per cent of the vote.

Today, Egypt's military deep state enjoys a completely free hand. Justice has been compromised, with a new Protest Law and Terrorism Law allowing for almost anyone to be labelled a revolutionary and tried in military rather than civilian courts, and the constitution has been rewritten to give the judiciary power to dissolve parliament at will. The president, meanwhile, remains outside the courts' jurisdiction. In case parliament does try to assert itself, the deep state has packed it with a cadre of former military, secret service and police officers. They comprise around 15 per cent of MPs, a significant and unified bloc in the face of the many other small and disunited parties represented in Egypt's parliament – sometimes as many as 20 at a time.

This political fragmentation allows Sisi – who has no party affiliation – to present himself as a presidential-monarch figure above parliamentary squabbles. After the near-miss of the Arab Spring and the fall of Mubarak, Egypt's military deep state is now very much back in control.

TURKEY

Sitting at the crossroads of Europe and Asia, Turkey has an identity problem. When he took over the country in 1923, following the Young Ottoman and Young Turk eras (see pp.24–8), Mustafa Kemal Atatürk wanted the newly created Republic of Turkey to be a secular, westward-looking nation – which it was until the millennium, when Islam-influenced political parties began to exercise power in Turkey for the first time.

This secular-Islamic split forms the backdrop to the deep state struggles that afflict the country today. But, being Turkey, it's more complex than that – Byzantine, you might say. While secular, Westernizing 'Kemalism' is in decline as a military and political force in Turkey, in part brought low by its deep state involvement in organized crime, drug trafficking and corruption, the Islamic equivalents that have replaced it are equally compromised by their misuse of power and by internal divisions that contributed to the failed military coup of 2016. According to your deep-state conspiracy theory of choice, this coup was either real or staged, and was launched by either vengeful Kemalists or discontented Islamists – or both.

Turkey looks west

When Atatürk died in 1938, Turkey was set on its path towards Westernization. Religious clothing had been banned, use of the Latin alphabet was enforced and the army was charged, by law, to 'protect and keep watch over the Republic'. It was a mission the armed forces would zealously prosecute, launching coups in 1960, 1971 and 1980 when it felt the country's rulers were straying too far from Atatürk's westward path. In each instance the military eventually handed power back to civilian governments. It had other matters to attend to, not least its involvement in large-scale drug trafficking with its business partners in organized crime.

It was while campaigning against Kurdish and Armenian separatists in the 1970s that corrupt elements within the armed forces hierarchy first noticed that the conflict zones they operated in also contained many of Turkey's narcotics production and transportation areas. It was a trade worth an estimated US$50 billion a year and the military deep state wanted in, partnering with some drug cartels and initiating 'dirty wars' against others. With a lucrative sideline in narcotics and a political class fully aware of its subservient position to the military, the Kemalist consensus appeared settled.

This changed in 1980, when a sharp rise in far-left protests against a weak coalition government provoked the military to launch another coup. Ordinarily, the armed forces would have jailed the leading protestors, imposed order and then restored parliamentary government, but on this occasion the coup leader General Kenan Evren saw there was a bigger issue in play, namely the rise of communism as an ideology in Turkey. His solution to counteract this was to relax the country's stringent secularist laws and inculcate the Islamic faith into young people by introducing mandatory religious lessons at school. Evren's military junta also embraced the newly fashionable free-market economics that many Western nations practised. For Turkey, this meant allowing market access to Muslim entrepreneurs previously excluded by a closed shop of secular business leaders through their Turkish Industry and Business Association (TUSIAD).

A key figure who took advantage of Turkey's new religious tolerance was the scholar, mystic and activist Fethullah Gülen. A Muslim fundamentalist, he encouraged his many followers to enlist in the military, enter politics, join the civil service and sign up to the judiciary so that they could Islamicize Turkey from within. In short, Gülen planned to replace the Kemalist deep state with an Islamic one. Ordinarily, this process would have taken decades, but in the mid-1990s an event occurred that exposed the political and military corruption among Turkey's ruling elite and led Gülen to fast-track his plans – in partnership with a political rising star who would prove to be his nemesis.

It all comes crashing down

It was known as the Susurluk Scandal and was precipitated by a fatal car crash outside the town of that name on 3 November 1996. The vehicle, a Mercedes 600 SEL, was driven by Sedat Bucak, an MP and pro-Turkey Kurdish tribal leader. Bucak survived the accident but his three passengers were all killed. They were Hüseyin Kocadağ, Istanbul's deputy chief of police, Gonca Us, a model and beauty pageant contestant, and Abdullah Çatlı, a notorious far-right militant, drug trafficker and contract killer. In the car's boot were thousands of US dollars, several weapons, two listening devices, a fake passport for Çatlı and a stash of narcotics. When it was later revealed that the car's brakes had been tampered with, the crash investigation turned into a murder inquiry, with rival drug gangs, rogue military units and crooked politicians cited as possible suspects. Turkey's press, attempting to make sense of the case's many curious details – not least what brought this unusual quartet together – invented a new term to describe the institutions and actors involved: *derin devlet*, or 'deep state'. Although the concept of a deep state had been around for millennia, this was the first time it had been named. Turkey's dirty little deep state secret was out in the open, and as well as those killed in the Susurluk crash another victim of the incident was the secular, Kemalist consensus that had allowed state-sponsored crime and corruption to flourish.

Over the next few years, establishment figures implicated in deep-state activity were turned out of office – and replaced with Gülenists ready to push their own Islamic deep-state agenda. In this, they would be helped from 2001 by the formation of a new Islamic political party, AKP (Adalet ve Kalkınma Partisi, or Justice

Islamic radical Fethullah Gülen helped end Turkey's Kemalist consensus – only to be outmanoeuvred by one-time ally Recep Erdoğan.

and Development Party) led by the former mayor of Istanbul, Recep Tayyip Erdoğan.

Erdoğan's end game

Erdoğan said his party would offer transparency and accountability, promising that the Susurluk Scandal's details would 'be exposed in all their nakedness'. On becoming Turkey's prime minister in 2002, he launched what became known as the Ergenekon investigation into the ultra-nationalist deep-state network of military and secret service officers. This probe was ramped up when the military allegedly tried to organize a coup after the 2007 presidential election was won by the AKP candidate Abdullah Gül. By 2012, as the Ergenekon investigation wound down, 300 alleged conspirators had been convicted as members of anti-state terrorist organizations and hundreds more high-ranking military men had been hounded out of the armed forces. The Gülenists' infiltration of the civil service and judiciary allowed them to root out 'traitors' there too.

By 2013, with new presidential elections just a year away and Erdoğan announcing his intention to stand, it appeared that Fethullah Gülen's dream of a Muslim-led takeover of the state was becoming a reality. But the Gülenists were about to have their hopes dashed. They had helped Erdoğan get where he wanted to be, and now he decided it was time to cut them loose.

Although the AKP and the Gülenists were both Islamic in outlook, they practised their faith in very different ways. For Fethullah Gülen, Islam was a spiritual journey of personal growth; for Erdoğan, it was a conservative belief that preached order and obedience – particularly obedience to him. In Erdoğan's ideology there was no room for a potential rival such as Gülen.

Relations began to sour in early 2013 when Gülenists joined protests in Istanbul against Erdoğan-approved plans to close and redevelop the city's popular Gezi Park. The AKP leader hit back at the Gülenists' 'people over profits' rhetoric by closing down some of their business interests. Things escalated rapidly from there. The Gülenists retaliated by publicizing details of wide-ranging corruption in Erdoğan's cabinet and illegal government arms shipments to Syria, to which the government responded by closing down Gülenist-run schools and labelling Hizmet, Gülen's political movement, a terrorist organization. Erdoğan won the 2014 presidential election but was immediately in trouble. Having cleansed the military, bureaucracy and judiciary of most of its Kemalist deep-state elements, he now had to reckon with the Gülenist shadow state that had replaced it.

The attempted military coup against Erdoğan in 2016 was launched by an uneasy alliance of remaining Kemalists and the president's former Gülenist allies. Luckily for Erdoğan, the lack of coordination between these two camps caused the coup to fail, though it was a close-run thing. Nevertheless, having survived the rebellion Erdoğan used it to effect a Stalinist-style cull of his enemies. Every single member of Turkey's judiciary was placed under investigation following the failed coup. Thirty per cent of the country's top generals were sacked and detained. More than 115,000 people lost their jobs or were suspended, including 10,000 members of the armed forces, 3,000 judges and prosecutors, and more than 35,000 civil servants. A similar number of teachers had their contracts terminated and every single one of the country's 1,577 university deans was forced to resign. Fifteen universities, 1,000 private schools, and more than 1,200 charities and foundations with alleged Kemalist and Gülenist links were closed and had their assets seized. One hundred and sixty media and publishing outlets were shut. Forty-eight journalists were arrested and hundreds lost their accreditation.

In April 2017, President Erdoğan narrowly won a national referendum to change Turkey's constitution, abolish the office of prime minister, limit the authority of parliament and boost the power of the president. Now a dictator in all but name, Erdoğan had taken on and defeated not one deep state, but two. Ultimately, Erdoğan was less interested in the Gülenists' religious dream of

A demonstration in support of President Erdoğan, shortly after the coup attempt in 2016.

restoring the Muslim Caliphate to Turkey than in reviving his country's Ottoman Empire glories as the Middle East's major regional power. With neighbouring Syria and Iraq in turmoil, and Iran a pariah state, the opportunity is certainly there – though the United States and Russia, not to mention Saudi Arabia and Israel, will no doubt demand a say in matters as Erdoğan's strategy evolves.

CHAPTER 4
ASIA

THE DEEP STATES of Asia usually wear uniforms, but individual militaries like to put their own stamp on things. Pakistan, for example, represents a 'classic' deep state that uses the threat of military intervention to keep its politicians in line. Thailand's secret rulers, on the other hand, have adopted a subtler approach by re-engineering the machinery of government in their favour – and with public approval. Myanmar has seen a powerful military retreat from the role of running the country, but only so that it can exercise true power as a shadow government and narco-state. As for North Korea, the possible existence of a military deep state there may cause us to reconsider everything we think we know about this strange and secretive country.

PAKISTAN

When Imran Khan was elected Pakistan's prime minister in August 2018, it was the culmination of a successful campaign by the military deep state to put in power the candidate it thought it could best control.

Pakistan's history since gaining independence in 1947 is one of troubled spells of civilian government – left-wing, conservative, religious – interspersed with periods of military rule. On the whole, Pakistan's military deep state avoids the bother of actually running the country to focus instead on advancing its own agenda. Unlike many other deep states, this does not mean the theft of riches from the public purse; Pakistan's deep state is more interested in other pursuits. First, it wants to protect its pre-eminent position. Pakistan's armed forces are the seventh largest globally and the only forces in the Muslim world in possession of nuclear weapons. Twenty per cent of the country's annual budget is consumed by the military, and as a developing but still relatively poor nation this is a disproportionately high figure that the armed forces are not inclined to see reduced by a single penny. Secondly, Pakistan's military in general and its deep state in particular are ideologically committed to advancing an anti-Indian and Pakistan-first agenda that the country's government is unwilling to pursue openly.

A successful campaign

This is why a former playboy and cricket-star-turned-politician as a candidate for prime minister was such a blessing for Pakistan's military elites. Imran Khan was a political novice leading a fairly new party. By helping Khan become prime minister Pakistan's deep state believed he would be forever in their debt, if not their pocket.

Pakistan's generals approached the 2018 election with military precision. First, the media was intimidated into limiting its coverage of Imran Khan's political opponents. Although this resulted in a pro-free speech petition signed by 50 of the country's best-known journalists, it was a request (or threat) that the TV and press adhered to. Next, the military targeted the Muslim League, the biggest electoral challenger to Khan's Pakistan Movement for Justice (PMJ). To this end, the former prime minister and Muslim

League leader Nawaz Sharif, who remained immensely popular despite his removal from office in 2017 on a corruption charge, was unceremoniously jailed and barred from receiving visitors.

With the media gagged and the Muslim League's most popular leader sequestered, the military declared that it would oversee the running of the election. This resulted in voter intimidation at polling stations, missing ballot boxes in Muslim League strongholds, and international electoral observers denied access to politically marginal areas. In one now-notorious video circulated after the election, votes for rival parties were shown being added to the PMJ tally. To make doubly sure of a Khan victory, the deep state also promoted a number of extremist and fringe political parties to split the Muslim League vote, most notoriously Harkat-ul-Jihad, a group declared a terrorist organization by the UN.

Imran Khan's electoral victory was modest – a fact that also worked in the deep state's favour. Khan had not sought the army's support and certainly did not want to be dependent on it, but as the inexperienced leader of a fragile coalition government that was exactly the position he found himself in.

Playing both sides

The deep state's dealings with outlawed groups such as Harkat-ul-Jihad was not an isolated incident. Since the 1980s and maybe earlier, Pakistan's military, operating in a rogue capacity at odds with official government policy, has fostered and funded regional fundamentalist terrorist groups on a regular basis.

It began with the Soviet Union's invasion of Afghanistan in 1980. Alarmed at the prospect of Russian tanks and missiles on its western border, Pakistan's military secret police, the Inter-Service Intelligence (ISI), allied with the CIA to bankroll and arm Afghan mujahedin rebels against the invading Soviets. When the Russians finally pulled out of Afghanistan in the late 1980s, Pakistan's deep state continued to support Islamic fundamentalist groups in the country, reasoning that they would be useful clients to cultivate

Pakistan's Muslim League leader, Nawaz Sharif.

once a settled Afghan government tried to assert its own regional aspirations – which would no doubt conflict with neighbouring Pakistan's.

This 'my enemy's enemy is my friend' approach was one Pakistan's deep state applied elsewhere, especially in its efforts to undermine Indian power at any opportunity. It was only brought to an end, and then only temporarily, following the 9/11 attacks in 2001 and the ensuing and ongoing War on Terror launched by the United States and its allies – including Pakistan – against al-Qaeda, ISIS and their many offshoots. Pakistan's leader in 2001 was Pervez Musharraf, and, under pressure from the Americans, he purged the ISI leadership of its pro-fundamentalist elements. Musharraf could do this as he was an army man himself, having come to power in a military coup in 1999; it is questionable whether a civilian leader would have successfully taken this step.

Yet even Musharraf could only keep the ISI in line for a while and by 2005 it was up to its old dirty tricks, supporting an insurgent militia known as the Haqqani network that was targeting US-led NATO forces in Afghanistan. More overtly, the ISI was behind a July 2008 suicide bomb attack on the Indian embassy in Afghanistan that killed at least 50 people. In November that same year, Islamic terrorists launched a three-day assault on Mumbai in India that a later US intelligence report linked to the ISI. One outcome of this was a lawsuit filed in 2010 by families of American victims against Lieutenant General Ahmed Shuja Pasha, the ISI chief, for complicity in the attack.

With each passing year, America's belief in the reliability of Pakistan's military diminished, finally reaching vanishing point with the 'Geronimo' operation of 2 May 2011. This was the Navy SEAL mission that killed Osama bin Laden in his hideout in a suburb of the garrison city of Abbottabad, about 60 km (37 miles) north-east of Islamabad. Fearful that bin Laden would be tipped off by the military deep state, the US launched the attack without informing Pakistan's government. It was assumed, probably correctly, that the ISI already knew of bin Laden's whereabouts. After all, he had been living in a lightly guarded compound less than a mile from a Pakistani military academy for six years. In those circumstances, it was understandable that Barack Obama, in authorizing the secret attack, was more prepared to suffer the righteous indignation of Pakistan's government than risk the success of the mission by being honest with them about it.

In preferencing its own agenda of cultivating potentially useful but uncompromisingly violent Islamic fundamentalist groups over the War on Terror designed to destroy them, Pakistan's deep state is playing a dangerous double game. While it does not fear its own country's civilian politicians, it is wary of retribution by the United States. This would most likely mean the withdrawal of the generous funding Pakistan's armed forces receive from America, at least US$12 billion since 2011. Ultimately, Pakistan's deep state is banking on the US deciding that it needs its support, come what may.

The other side of this coin is that Pakistan's military needs to be careful with whom it associates. In recent years, some of the terrorist groups that Pakistan's deep state has directed against Afghani and Indian interests have turned their attentions to their former handlers and they are growing in power in a Pakistan they see as America's stooge. This, in part, explains the army's support for Imran Khan in 2018. With a moderate, practically secular leader they can direct in office, Pakistan's deep state is seeking to keep control of the country's political direction.

THAILAND

Once a country where its monarch reigned supreme, Thailand is now experiencing an uneven and contested transition towards democracy. Whether and how it gets there depends on how the Thai army navigates this change. As the democratic impulse grows in Thailand, with reform and people-power movements active in ways that were once unthinkable, the military deep state has been forced to reconsider how it tackles dissent. In the old days, brute force was enough. Today, the army is experimenting with taking the parliamentary road to domination, with some success.

The rise of the military

Thailand, then called Siam, became a parliamentary democracy in 1932. What propelled Siam's army to prominence alongside its politicians was World War II – or, rather, the Cold War that broke out immediately after it. As China, North Korea, Laos and North Vietnam all succumbed to insurgent communist regimes, free world nations, especially the US, pushed back. Marxist-resistant states, such as Siam (officially renamed Thailand in 1949), were plied with money, arms and military assistance to turn them into bulwarks against the rising red tide.

Suddenly, Thailand's military was a major player. This was particularly true for a division of the Thai army known as the Communist Suppression Operations Command (CSOC). Initially established to combat far-left groups within Thailand, in time the CSOC widened its remit to become the political wing of the armed forces. In 1974 it was redesignated as the Internal Security Operations Command (ISOC) and given the powers that the 'internal security' part of its name implied. In short, ISOC was the executive arm of Thailand's deep state.

Backed by American money and with CSOC/ISOC providing the muscle, the Thai army appointed itself the ultimate arbiter in the country's political life. It tolerated the country's parliamentary system, but, when it felt that Thailand's democracy was becoming *too* democratic, it stepped in, seized power, purged parliament, and then handed – or rather loaned – power back to the politicians.

Mobilizing the masses

Coups in 1947, 1948, 1977 and 1991 served to remind Thailand's political leaders who was really in charge, but the election of the telecoms and media billionaire Thaksin Shinawatra in 2001 changed

A meeting of Thailand's Internal Security Operations Command (ISOC).

the game. Shinawatra was an unashamed populist with huge appeal, especially among Thailand's poor rural population, and could in time have feasibly amassed enough power to genuinely threaten the military's hegemony. This was certainly the case in 2005, when Shinawatra became the first democratically elected Thai politician to both serve out a full term and be re-elected.

For the deep state, Shinawatra's unprecedented electoral success was a declaration of war – but before removing the prime minister, the military had first to undermine him. They did this by focusing on Shinawatra's extensive business interests.

Once Shinawatra became prime minister, he and his wife, Potjaman, were obliged by law to divest themselves of any shares in the large corporation they owned. Known as Shin, it ran mobile phone networks, Thai TV stations, satellite broadcast services and other media operations. In compliance with the letter, if not the spirit, of the law the Shinawatras did indeed offload their shares – to their children and to Potjaman's brother, Banpot Damapong, a technical sleight of hand that was decried by Thaksin Shinawatra's opponents. More denunciations followed when it was revealed that the prime minister had transferred millions of dollars in shares to his domestic staff, including a housemaid, a security guard and a chauffeur. An investigation was launched, and Shinawatra was cleared in late 2001 after claiming he had made 'an honest mistake' by not declaring the generous gift he had made to his employees.

From there on, Thaksin Shinawatra faced constant accusations that his political position and his family's commercial activities constituted a conflict of interest. This included claims of graft and negligence over the approval of a lottery scheme in 2003 and reports that his family business had benefited when the prime minister ordered Thailand's Export-Import Bank to loan money to a Myanmar-based company that needed financing in order to buy a Shinawatra family-owned satellite communications company.

Finally, in early 2006, the whole Shinawatra clan and Banpot Damapong sold off their shares in Shin to a Singapore-based rival for US$2 billion. This was a win-win for the military deep state, which wasted no time in pointing out that the Shinawatras had enjoyed five full years of political-commercial collusion and then topped it off with a US$2 billion windfall. Almost overnight a nationalist, pro-military and royalist anti-Shinawatra movement known as the Yellow Shirts sprang up to protest in noisy street demonstrations against alleged corruption. But despite appearances, the Yellow Shirts was not a spontaneously generated grassroots movement; the organization was in fact co-founded by the former governor of Bangkok, Major General Chamlong Srimuang. Shinawatra had given the deep state the excuse it needed and now it was mobilizing against him.

Mass public protests on the streets of Bangkok shut down the capital as the Yellow Shirts noisily accused Shinawatra of graft, abuse of power and – a serious accusation in Thailand – disrespecting the king. With the prime minister suitably embattled, the deep state tried its luck. In late August 2006 an army lieutenant named

Thawatchai Klinchana was arrested outside Shinawatra's residence in a car containing around 40 kg (88 lb) of high explosives. As well as being an army officer, Klinchana had direct links to the deep state, having formerly been the driver for ISOC deputy director Pallop Pinmanne. Although Shinawatra fought back, sacking Pinmanne for example, the failed assassination attempt only stiffened the deep state's resolve. Just three weeks after the failed bomb plot, Thaksin Shinawatra was ousted from office in a military coup.

Two years later, he was convicted *in absentia* over his supposed involvement in a corrupt land deal. In more recent times, the old

An anti-Shinawatra Yellow Shirts rally in Bangkok, 2008.

lottery and Export-Import Bank charges have been revived against the former prime minister, who now lives in exile in Dubai and maintains that any allegations and convictions he suffers are all politically motivated. Whatever the truth, Thailand's military deep state-controlled courts do appear to be particularly obsessed with the Shinawatras, as in 2017 Panthongtae Shinawatra, Thaksin's only son, was charged with money laundering in a case involving 9.9 billion Thai baht (US$294 million).

With Shinawatra gone and his reputation tarnished, the deep state hoped things would calm down. Instead, an anti-military and pro-Shinawatra mass movement known as the Red Shirts developed. This populist reaction to the 2006 coup presented the military deep state with a conundrum that it would spend the next decade resolving.

That there was still deep state work to do became obvious after the Shinawatra-aligned People's Power Party won the military junta-sanctioned general election of December 2007. The generals reacted by accusing the People's Power Party of electoral fraud and, in what was later dubbed a judicial coup, had the organization dissolved by Thailand's Constitutional Court. For the next few years a succession of weak coalition governments came and went as the deep state searched for a more effective answer to the problem of populism.

Doing it by the book

When the deep state did devise an alternative to its old 'coup and replace' policy it needed to launch one more military takeover in order to effect it. In a neat piece of political drama, the unlucky prime minister it turned out of office in May 2014 was Yingluck Shinawatra, Thaksin Shinawatra's sister. (Given the armed forces' history with her family, there was little surprise when, in 2017, Yingluck Shinawatra was handed a five-year sentence *in absentia* for negligence and mismanaging a government rice subsidy scheme – proof, some said, of the Shinawatra clan's incorrigible dishonesty, or, for others, an instance of the deep state's unending vendetta against the family that it sees as its most powerful rival.)

The 2014 coup was led by General Prayut Chan-o-cha, and over the next five years he and his allies set about reorganizing Thailand's parliamentary system to make their position unassailable. First, they introduced a complicated form of proportional representation that virtually ensured every election would result in weak and fractious coalition governments. They then amended the constitution so that all 250 members of parliament's upper house, the Senate, were appointed by the military. In a carefully stage-managed referendum, the deep state submitted a draft of the new constitution to the people. As a precaution, anti-amendment campaigns were banned, protesters were jailed in the run-up to the ballot and independent observers were denied access to polling stations on the day of the vote. Although the turnout was low, around 55 per cent, two-thirds of voters approved the new, pro-deep state constitution.

In March 2019, Thailand's military rulers put these new judicial and political arrangements to the test in a general election contested by 77 parties. General Prayut, having led the 2014 coup, resigned his army role and stood as a parliamentary candidate at the head of the new Palang Pracharath Party, which took 116 of the 500 available lower house places. Its main rival, the Shinawatra-aligned Pheu Thai Party, amassed 136 seats. Pheu Thai would probably have garnered more MPs if the army-appointed Election Commission had not dismissed opposition accusations of electoral fraud, voter intimidation and miscounting by Prayut's backers. Despite this setback, Pheu Thai tried to form a government at the head of a seven-party coalition. The deep state-controlled Constitutional Court struck this down, too. As planned, the military's strategy for a legalized seizure of power was coming together perfectly. The endgame arrived when the heavily compromised Senate was called in to break the deadlock and duly appointed its patron Prayut Chan-o-cha as prime minister.

MYANMAR

In 2010, after 60 years of military dictatorship, Myanmar – the former British colony of Burma – began a peaceful and orderly transition towards democracy. It was hailed as a triumph of people power over the generals, evidence of the unstoppable march of freedom against oppression. More specifically, the event celebrated the heroism and fortitude of Myanmar's most famous dissident, the pro-democracy campaigner Aung San Suu Kyi.

In reality, 2010 represented none of those things. Rather, it marked the submersion of Myanmar's deep state after 60 years of uncontested rule, a retreat into the shadows from where it could more privately direct the country's fate without accountability.

Taking a back seat

Like any good deep state, Myanmar's military understood the difference between running a country and exercising power. The former is an onerous and often thankless task of endless administration and problem-solving; the latter is where true authority lies – and where the money is. By outsourcing the burdens of office, the military deep state was free to concentrate on the more lucrative pursuits of managing its many business interests and overseeing Myanmar's ever-growing drugs trade, safe in the knowledge that the country's civilian government could not lift a finger to stop it.

This has placed figures such as Aung San Suu Kyi in a figurative straitjacket. In 2016, the most iconic opponent of the old military regime was appointed as Myanmar's state counsellor (a kind of unofficial prime minister) and soon found that she had become the front person for a regime over which she had little control. It's one reason why the revered Nobel Peace Prize laureate of 1991 is now widely reviled. Her failure to fix Myanmar's economic woes and her inaction, at best, over the army's ongoing oppression of the Muslim Rohingya people of western Myanmar – 'a textbook example of ethnic cleansing', according to the UN – has fatally undermined her standing both at home and abroad.

In retrospect, her appointment was a clever ploy by the deep state. In election after election since the 2010 transition, Aung San Suu Kyi's NLD party has won landslide victories but has been unable to translate electoral support into effective action. The terms of the 2010 transition ensure this. The ministries of defence, home affairs and border affairs all remain under military control, for example, while 25 per cent of the seats in parliament are reserved for the armed forces. This, along with the deep state's wider powers of control and coercion, prevents Aung San Suu Kyi from enacting any meaningfully progressive legislation and simultaneously eats away at her reputation.

The embodiment of the deep state's 'wider powers' is Senior-General Than Shwe. When he retired in 2011, Than Shwe had been the uncontested leader of Myanmar's ruling military junta for 20 years. His departure left a huge power vacuum that only one man could fill: Than Shwe himself. After all, dictators don't retire and Than Shwe is no exception. From his comfortable estate in the capital city of Naypyidaw, the famously taciturn and tactical general continues to exert considerable influence, no doubt utilizing his skills as an army psy-ops practitioner, politics instructor and keen chess player. Dignitaries from neighbouring China and Thailand discuss foreign policy strategy with him, while Myanmar's military and political leaders – including Aung San Suu Kyi – regularly pay court to the octogenarian statesman.

With Than Shwe pulling the strings and with military officers embedded in parliament and in the cabinet, and with Aung San Suu Kyi in place as a human shield to absorb criticism, Myanmar's deep state is free to get on with what it does best: feathering its own nest.

Until the late 1980s Myanmar was a socialist republic, but in 1988 it abruptly switched to a policy of state-led capitalism. From that point on, the deep state has made sure it receives its cut of any commercial enterprise operating in the country. All foreign investors, for example, have to enter into joint ventures with

The power behind Myanmar's throne, Than Shwe is the embodiment of his nation's military deep state.

military firms as a precondition to doing business in Myanmar. In 1990 the armed forces expanded their commercial interests by setting up two huge corporations: the Union of Myanmar Economic Holdings (UMEH) and the Myanmar Economic Corporation (MEC). These organizations remain under military control today and hand out lucrative contracts to the highest bidder for large state building projects, infrastructure schemes and the exploitation of Myanmar's copious natural resources of jade, rubber, timber, oil and gas. Bribes, or 'tea money', are freely exchanged and cronyism and nepotism is rife.

No war on drugs

Beyond the deep state's forays into commerce, Myanmar's military leaders are heavily involved in the narcotics trade. This takes the form of giving legal impunity to drug producers and traffickers, laundering money through state-run businesses and banks, and providing investment opportunities for drug barons in government-controlled commercial enterprises. Heroin was traditionally the drug of choice for the region's producers, but in recent times it's been augmented by an expansion into synthetics such as crystal methamphetamine, or ice, exported to China, Australia, Japan and South Korea. According to the United Nations Office on Drugs and Crime (UNODC), Myanmar's narcotics trade is worth US$60 billion a year.

A complicating factor is that Myanmar's drugs are produced in the country's borderlands, where ethnic and tribal separatist groups have long been at war with the central government, especially in the wild and mountainous Shan State bordering China and Thailand. However, displaying the strategic nous for which it is rightly famed, Myanmar's deep state simply offered to end the fighting and allow the insurgents a degree of autonomy in return for a stake in the heroin and crystal meth trade.

With the might of Myanmar's military deep state behind them, the drug traffickers became untouchable. In 2005, for example,

American courts indicted eight Shan State narco-lords but Myanmar's military rulers refused to extradite them. Why would they? With drug money laundered through state-run banks (which cream off a 25 per cent 'whitening tax'), business is too good. Dirty money is also washed through a real-estate investment racket whereby traffickers pay above the market price for properties and the state legitimizes the sale and pockets the difference. This is an accusation levelled at Asia World Company, for example, Myanmar's largest real-estate investor. Its chairman Lo Ping Zhong, also known as Steven Law, is wanted in the US on drug-trafficking and money-laundering charges, and is the son of Lo Hsing Han, one of Myanmar's biggest drug lords. Nevertheless, Asia World Company works closely with Myanmar's military in many of its real-estate developments and building projects. So common is the legitimization of narco-money through state-run businesses that, according to one expert on the region, 'the directory of Myanmar's Chamber of Commerce and Industry reads like a who's who in the drug trade'.

With so many business interests to look after, it's no surprise that Myanmar's deep state was eager to relinquish control of the country in 2010. For Myanmar's military elites, looting the country is a much more rewarding activity than running it.

NORTH KOREA

When Kim Jong-un disappeared for six weeks in 2014, North Korea watchers were perplexed. Was the Supreme Leader ill, or dead? Surely he hadn't been deposed by the army? The Kim family had ruled North Korea since 1948, building an impregnable personality cult around each successive leader. Opposition to the Kims simply did not exist.

Kim Jong-un's return to office in October 2014 confirmed that he was still very much alive and in charge. He had been ill, his people explained. Of course there had been no coup. The loyalty of the military was not in question. And yet . . .

Discord in the family

The first mention of a North Korean deep state came in 2004, via the defector Jang Jin-sung, the country's former chief propagandist. Jang had been a close confidant of Kim Jong-un's father and predecessor, Kim Jong-il. In Jang's telling, the deep state was born when Kim Jong-il took a small, administrative department within the armed forces bureaucracy and transformed it into his personal Praetorian Guard. It was called the Organization and Guidance Department (OGD) and Kim Jong-il first enlisted its services during the latter years of his father Kim Il-sung's dictatorship. Kim Il-sung had taken control of North Korea in 1948, establishing it as the repressive Stalinist state that it remains today. But by the early 1990s the ageing 'Eternal President of the Republic' was worn out and possibly senile. According to Jang Jin-sung, Kim Jong-il ordered the OGD to place his father in isolation and keep his true condition top secret – not just from the outside world but from the country's military and political hierarchy. When Kim Il-sung died in 1994, Kim Jong-il rewarded the OGD with power and privilege for services rendered. In return, the OGD remained unswervingly loyal until Kim Jong-il's death in 2011.

Two narrative streams emerge at this point. In the first version, Kim Jong-un succeeded his father as North Korea's absolute and uncontested ruler. In the second, deep state story, the OGD decided that Kim Jong-un, still in his late twenties, was not dictator material and that its time had come. The OGD allowed Kim to assume the role of leader, but kept true power for itself.

With North Korea being perhaps the most closed nation on Earth, it is impossible to verify which of these stories is true. What is clear is that for every argument supporting Kim's total authority there is an equally strong counter-argument that the OGD is really in charge. Consider the fate of Jang Song-thaek in 2013, barely two years into Kim's reign. Jang was Kim's uncle by marriage and an influential political figure. This also made him a potential rival and it's why, deep-state deniers say, the Supreme

Leader had him executed – proof, if needed, of Kim's strong and decisive authority.

The opposite argument is that the deep state took out Jang. After all, why would Kim murder his own uncle, a trusted advisor and a close confidant of his dead father? It was Jang's links to Kim Jong-il, the counter-story goes, that ensured his demise. Jang knew where the OGD buried its bodies – which is why he ended up as one of them. Also, the removal of Jang allowed the OGD to tighten its hold on Kim.

Similarly, in the deep-state narrative, Kim Jong-un's mysterious six-week disappearance in 2014 was not due to illness, as claimed. He may have been a puppet, but he was also a Kim – and as such was an implacable enemy of South Korea. So, was it a coincidence that, with Kim Jong-un incapacitated in September 2014, North Korean officials – including OGD members – met with South Korean representatives for the first time in many years and agreed to open a line of dialogue with their supposed enemies? Was the deep state, weary of decades of international isolation and under-development, planning for peace and reconciliation with the outside world? If it was, Kim Jong-un, a living example of North Korean totalitarianism, would be the ideal sacrificial lamb when the time came for the country to transition from pariah state to something approaching a democracy. It's no surprise, then, that he was not invited to the secret North–South talks.

Then there is the shocking and bizarre assassination of Kim Jong-un's half-brother, Kim Jong-nam, in 2017, when he was publicly poisoned at Kuala Lumpur Airport in Malaysia. Kim Jong-nam had been Kim Jong-il's designated heir before falling out with his father in 2001 and fleeing into exile – an event that ultimately led to Kim Jong-un's rise to power. So long as Kim Jong-nam remained a 'king over the water', anti-deep staters argue, Kim Jong-un's legitimacy would always be questioned. Yet in the pro-deep state version Kim Jong-nam – the former Supreme Leader's son, no less – was openly executed as a warning to other high-profile defectors not to criticize the country. In the aftermath of the attack several prominent North Korean exiles, including Thae Yong-ho, the former ambassador to Great Britain, did indeed go into hiding and stop their attacks on the state. It should also be remembered that there were two earlier unsuccessful attempts on Kim Jong-nam's life, the first in 2010, a year before Kim Jong-un came to power.

Mr Deep State?

The most fascinating 'evidence' of deep-state influence in North Korea is the career of Choe Ryong-hae. Choe has been active in high-level North Korean politics since the early 1990s and ran the ODG for many years. It is possible that he still does. He was once a close associate of Jang Song-thaek and of many other North Korean generals and party leaders who have since been fired or executed. Yet Choe has thrived and prospered. And, depending on your deep-state preference, this is because Kim either trusts or fears him.

When Kim Jong-un found himself in an increasingly heated squabble with Donald Trump in 2017 over North Korea's nuclear missile development programme, it was Choe who stepped in and calmed things down – taking the opportunity in the process to demote (or worse) several influential generals accused of not wholeheartedly supporting Kim's anti-American posturing. Among those removed by Choe was General Hwang Pyong-so, one of Kim's trusted advisors, and, therefore, an impediment to Choe and the ODG's deep state influence.

Ascending ever upwards, in April 2019 Choe was announced President of the Presidium of the Supreme People's Assembly of North Korea – in other words, the deep state was now the head of state.

A criminal enterprise

So, if North Korea does have a deep state, what does it do all day? Mostly, it looks at ways to make money.

Follower or leader? Choe Ryong-hae may well be the man that really runs North Korea.

North Korea is a poor country. For decades it relied on handouts from the Soviet Union to keep it afloat, but the fall of communism after 1989 put paid to that. China also supplied cash and aid, but North Korea would ideally prefer not to be reliant on a single benefactor, especially a large and predatory one camped on its northern border.

In addition, a history of poor economic planning, mis-management, corruption and stifling international sanctions means that North Korea is pretty much the last country international businesses think of when deciding where to invest their capital. In response, North Korea has turned itself into a centre of excellence for illegal commerce. Today, the country is a leading producer of crystal methamphetamine, fentanyl (a potent form of synthetic heroin) and fake Viagra. Cyber-crime is a particular growth industry. In 2016, for example, North Korean hackers almost stole US$1 billion from the US Federal Reserve and were only thwarted when an eagle-eyed official spotted a spelling mistake in one of their fake authorizations. In May 2016, North Korean ransomware also brought Britain's NHS to a standstill. It is estimated that state-sponsored criminality generates US$1–2 billion annually.

The government department overseeing all of this activity is known as Office 39. This 'ministry of crime' was set up by Kim Jong-il in 1994 to generate his own private slush fund, and reported directly to him. But, as with the ODG, it may be that control of Office 39 passed to the deep state on his death in 2011. As with everything else in North Korea the details of any link are opaque, but we do know that one of Office 39's top operatives is Choe Song – the son of none other than Choe Ryong-hae. Intriguingly, Choe Song is reportedly married to Kim Yo-jong, a rising star in the North Korean regime and the sister of Kim Jong-un. She is also thought to be a member of the ODG, and whether she is her brother's ally or potential rival remains to be seen. It may even be that the seemingly all-powerful Kim regime is slowly and stealthily being replaced by a putative Kim-Choe dynasty. In a country of secrets, it seems that the existence of North Korea's deep state may be its best-kept secret of all.

CHAPTER 5

AFRICA

ALL OF THE elements that deep-state actors thrive on are present on the continent of Africa, especially sub-Saharan Africa, the focus of this chapter. There is a troubled post-colonial legacy, economic underdevelopment, a democratic deficit, political instability and seemingly limitless natural resources to be exploited. It has created a situation where corruption is commonplace and where regional, ethnic and tribal affiliations count for more than grand political programmes aimed at making the region the economic powerhouse it ought to be. This suppression of Africa's potential is all to the benefit of the multinational corporations and large businesses with major interests there. And, as we shall see with the Republic of the Congo, Nigeria and South Africa, it's a benefit corporate deep states in particular have enthusiastically cashed in on.

Imperialism also has its role to play in the continent's susceptibility to deep state interference. While Britain and France are historically the main culprits in Africa (with Belgium receiving a dishonourable mention for its treatment of the Congo), the example we'll look at here is the modern-day covert colonialism of China's influence over Zimbabwe.

THE CONGO AND KATANGA

The country today called the Democratic Republic of the Congo lies at the heart of Africa and was formerly a Belgian colony. It was, and still is, one of the world's leading sources of copper, rubber, cobalt, tin and uranium, and for Belgium it was one enormous mine to be excavated mercilessly. It's one reason why Belgium simply packed up and left when the Congo won its independence in 1960, making little effort to effect an orderly transition from empire to republic. Belgium had lost an enormously valuable asset and was in no mood to leave with any grace.

But although Belgium had exited the new Republic of the Congo, many Belgians hadn't. The huge businesses that controlled the Congo's mining industry were almost entirely owned by Belgians, and they were not prepared to let independence obstruct the control they exerted over the country – or at least the part of it that mattered to them.

What's yours is mine

The Katanga region in south-east Congo is where most of the country's oil and gas reserves are and it's also where most of the foreign-run mining companies were based. The biggest and most influential of these was the Anglo-Belgian Union Minière du Haut-Katanga (Mining Union of Upper Katanga). Known as UM, the company's reach was so extensive it was virtually a state within a state. Like United Fruit in Guatemala (see pp.145–51), UM built railways, operated an employee healthcare programme, ran schools and hospitals and made sure that local leaders were firmly in its pocket. This was just as well, as UM and the region's other large foreign-owned businesses became alarmed when the newly independent Congolese government began making noises about nationalizing the mining industry. With their vast profits under threat, UM and its allies decided it was time for Katanga to go it alone. After recruiting local politician Moïse Tshombe as their front man, the mining cartels funded and set in motion a deep-state plot that left the country in turmoil and resulted in the death – and possibly murder – of the world's most senior diplomat, United Nations' Secretary-General Dag Hammarskjöld.

Just two weeks after the Republic of Congo was instituted on 30 June 1960, Moïse Tshombe unilaterally declared Katangan independence. This was followed by part of the neighbouring diamond-rich region of Kasai breaking away from Congo as the Mining State of South Kasai. Kasai was the stronghold of Forminière, another large Belgian mining group, who financed and directed the separatist movement. It is difficult to overstate the crippling effect these two secessions would have had on Congo's economy. UM taxes and duties alone accounted for more than

A Union Minière (UM) ore processing centre in Élisabethville (modern-day Lubumbashi, south-east Democratic Republic of the Congo), 1917.

50 per cent of Congo's annual revenue. Katanga's mines supplied 70 per cent of the world's cobalt and 60 per cent of its uranium, most notably for the atomic bombs dropped on Hiroshima and Nagasaki in 1945.

For its part, the Belgian government actively supported the Katanga and Kasai rebels. They sent in troops to help guard against 'unrest' and ordered their civil servants still in the region to stay in post and help stabilize Tshombe's regime. His treasury filled with UM money, Tshombe also began to recruit mercenaries from South Africa, Rhodesia and even the UK. These men were hardened killers and became known as *Les affreux* ('the dreadfuls'). Many were former French Foreign Legion soldiers, while others were ex-Wehrmacht and SS fighters. Arms and materiel were supplied by the Belgian government and by UM cash. UM also provided logistical support, allowing weapons and fighters to be shipped into Katanga via a copper-ore terminus it controlled in Angola and then transported in freight wagons running on UM-owned railroads.

With Belgium supporting the breakaway states, the Republic of Congo appealed for international help – and the Soviet Union gratefully obliged, inspired of course by anti-imperialist sentiment but also, possibly, by the potential future access to lots of weapons-grade uranium. Heightened Cold War tensions made it difficult for countries such as the US or the UK to take sides, even if they had wanted to. Both were inclined to follow the money and support the mining interests and the breakaway states, plus Katanga had valuable commercial links with British-controlled Rhodesia across its border that needed to be protected. So, with things at an impasse, the United Nations stepped in.

You win some, you lose some

Dag Hammarskjöld was an advocate of national sovereignty and supported Congolese independence and self-determination. He was more ambivalent about separatist movements such as those led by Moïse Tshombe, especially when backed and promoted by imperialist nations and corporate deep states. The UN had already issued a resolution, largely ignored, ordering all foreign mercenaries to leave Katanga when Hammarskjöld decided to take a more active role in the conflict. In September 1961 he announced he was flying to Katanga to broker a peace deal. He never made it. His plane crashed 14 km (9 miles) short of its destination, killing Hammarskjöld and all other 14 people on board. While this was a tragedy for the UN, the victims and their families, it was far from bad news for Moïse Tshombe and his deep-state backers. Any peace deal brokered by Hammarskjöld would certainly have involved an end to the independence of Katanga and Kasai, followed by a state takeover of the mining industry.

For years there has been speculation that Hammarskjöld's death was not an accident, and that Belgian business interests and Moïse Tshombe had been behind it. In 2016, a retired US National Security Agency (NSA) operative called Charles Southall claimed that on the night of Hammarskjöld's death he had listened in on radio traffic of a fighter pilot delivering a running commentary as he shot down an unarmed aircraft. Given the pilot's signal location, it could only have been Hammarskjöld's plane that he was describing. As the full transcripts of the radio messages remain classified, Southall's story has never been verified and an official UN investigation into the crash was inconclusive.

More clear-cut, however, was the reaction to Hammarskjöld's untimely passing. If the mining cartels and Tshombe thought his death would sabotage the peace talks they were correct, but for the wrong reasons. The UN under its new Secretary-General, U Thant, took a hard line with the separatists and vigorously supported military action against the rebels. By 1963, after much bloody fighting, Tshombe was forced to declare an end to the struggle. Katanga was reintegrated into the Republic of the Congo, as was Kasai. This was a massive setback for UM and the other Belgian corporations, and it only got worse when, in 1967, all of their mining interests were expropriated by the state. It took the Belgians several years to obtain any compensation from Congo, and what they received was nothing compared to the future incomes they had lost: UM was paid 7,750 million Belgian francs against a company value at the time of 16.2 billion Belgian francs (other estimates put the value as high as 40 billion Belgian francs). But by the time this happened much had changed in the country. It had been ruled since 1965 by the dictator Mobuto Sese Seko, who renamed the country Zaire in 1971 and stayed in power until he was ousted by a rebellion in 1997. The deep state was out; the one-party state was in.

Eventually, though, UM got over this loss. It turned its attention to other markets in Canada, the US, South America, Mexico, Spain and Iran, where its fortunes remained buoyant. In Congo/Zaire, the state-owned UM was renamed Gécamines and, deprived of its expert Belgian-based management, fared less well. Corruption and mismanagement meant that its profitability fell by up to 50 per cent in the post-deep-state era. A case of better the devil you know, perhaps?

NIGERIA

For decades, Shell has been the most active company in oil-rich Nigeria – too active for many, as the petrochemical giant has been the subject of several corruption investigations and deep-state allegations over the years. Many of these centre around the mid-1990s, when a military dictatorship led by General Sani Abacha ruled the country. This was something of a golden age of political corruption in Nigeria. In his five years in power, Abacha reputedly stole up to US$4 billion from the state coffers and allowed deep-state actors to compromise Nigeria's politicians and loot the country's economy. But fraud and dishonesty in Nigeria did not end with Abacha's death in 1998, and while the country's politicians come and go, Shell and other large oil companies have been a constant, and often controversial, presence.

The Shell game

Royal Dutch Shell has been operating in Nigeria since 1937, when the territory was still part of the British Empire. This British connection gave the Anglo-Dutch company special access to the corridors of power that it has maintained since Nigerian independence in 1960. Today, Shell has annual Nigerian oil and gas revenues of around US$4 billion, 7 per cent of its global turnover. In return, it contributes US$1 billion in taxes, fees and royalties to the Nigerian exchequer. Any threat to those revenues is cracked down upon decisively by Nigeria's government, but in one notorious episode from the 1990s Shell is also alleged to have contributed to the suppression of anti-oil dissent.

Nigeria's southern Ogoni region around the River Niger delta is rich in oil, which was bad news for the people who lived there when Shell and other petrochemical companies arrived in the 1970s. After years of expropriations, compulsory purchases and civil unrest, the Movement for the Survival of Ogoni People (MOSOP) was set up in 1990 to organize resistance to oil company influence. MOSOP's demands included US$6 billion in royalties from past oil production and US$4 billion for the environmental damage caused by the spillage of 40 million litres (nearly 9 million gallons) of oil into the delta each year, as well as the pollutants and acid rain caused by the gas burn-off associated with oil extraction. But there was violence too, with several attacks on oil company workers and properties. This led in 1993 to Shell and its partner companies ceasing all production in the Ogoni region in what was interpreted as a clear signal to the government to take action. In 1995, a year after the murder of four pro-government Ogoni leaders, Sani Abacha's military junta arrested, tried and hanged nine MOSOP activists for the crime, including the writer Ken Saro-Wiwa.

The executions provoked an international outcry, being seen as little more than the outcome of a show trial to discourage further regional dissent. Shell was thought to be involved in the

An oil refinery at Nembe Creek in the Niger delta.

affair, and, although it denied any liability, in November 1996 the company agreed a US$15 million settlement to the family of Ken Saro-Wiwa and others against claims it had collaborated in the trial and execution of the so-called Ogoni Nine. Later, two trial prosecution witnesses retracted their testimonies and claimed they had been bribed by Shell to lie under oath – an allegation they repeated in a Dutch courtroom in late 2019 as part of a lawsuit brought against Shell by Esther Kiobel, the widow of one of the Ogoni Nine.

This followed calls in 2017 by Amnesty International for a criminal investigation into Shell for complicity in human rights abuses including 'murder, rape and torture' carried out by the Nigerian military in the Ogoni region. According to witness statements published in the Amnesty report *A Criminal Enterprise?*, in the 1990s Shell managed a team of undercover police officers, trained by the Nigerian state security service, to carry out surveillance against its perceived enemies in the Ogoni lands. Of interest to true deep-state connoisseurs, one of the leaked papers acquired by Amnesty quoted Shell's head of security as saying: 'Each day I come to work . . . I will phone the director of state security. Exchange of information.'

According to Amnesty, 'Shell was running a shady undercover unit and then passing on information to the Nigerian security agency . . . The revelations show how close and insidious the relationship was between the oil company and the Nigerian state, and Shell has serious questions to answer.'

Infiltrating the state

Shell's troubles in Ogoni were not the only incident pointing to its possible deep-state influence. In 2010, Wikileaks published a cache of documents that appeared to show Shell actively operating inside the Nigerian government. The papers revealed that Shell had inserted operatives into all of the country's main ministries, and even joked that while the government had initially colluded in the infiltration the 'moles' had been in place so long that state officials had actually forgotten they were still there.

These assertions came from a number of leaked cables sent to US officials by Ann Pickard, Shell's vice-president for sub-Saharan Africa, and led to hasty denials by the company that this was indeed the case. In December 2010, Celestine AkpoBari of Social Action Nigeria was quoted in the *Guardian* newspaper as saying: 'Shell and the government of Nigeria are two sides of the same coin. Shell is everywhere. They have an eye and an ear in every ministry of Nigeria. They have people on the payroll in every community, which is why they get away with everything. They are more powerful than the Nigerian government.' The London-based watchdog Platform agreed. 'Shell claims to have nothing to do with Nigerian politics. In reality, Shell works deep inside the system, and has long exploited political channels in Nigeria to its own advantage.'

A very big deal

The Wikileaks revelations came at the same time as another corruption scandal emerged – one still going strong at the time of writing, after several regime changes and official pledges to end corruption.

In 2010, Shell and the Italian oil giant ENI purchased from Nigeria's government mining rights to the country's offshore Etan and Zabazaba oil fields. Known collectively as OPL 245, these fields contain 9 billion barrels of oil – a quarter of Nigeria's remaining reserves – plus an unspecified amount of natural gas. It was a great deal: Shell and ENI obtained a huge new asset, while Nigeria was richer to the tune of US$1.3 billion. The trouble was, none of that money found its way into Nigeria's treasury. Where that US$1.3 billion went – and whether Shell and ENI knew where it was going – is the subject of ongoing legal investigations in Nigeria, Holland and Italy.

In 1998, Nigeria's then oil minister Dan Etete clandestinely transferred ownership of the OPL 245 oil fields to a company called Malabu Oil & Gas. As Etete was a co-owner of Malabu this was at best ethically questionable and at worst wholly illegal, so it was no surprise that questions were asked when Shell and ENI bought the OPL 245 assets and Dan Etete suddenly became a very wealthy man. The Dutch and Italian fraud and corruption authorities were concerned enough to open up a joint investigation into the deal. Unsurprisingly, Shell and ENI claimed they had no idea of Malabu's disputed ownership of OPL 245 and said they had bought the oil fields in good faith from the Nigerian government. Holland's financial police were unconvinced and, in February 2016, raided Shell's HQ in the Hague and seized scores of documents and other data. The following year, Italian prosecutors filed legal papers showing that Shell's hierarchy was indeed aware, despite earlier protestations, that Malabu and Dan Etete were the end beneficiaries of the OPL 245 payment. In a public climb-down, a Shell spokesman explained, 'Over time it became clear to us that

Etete was involved in Malabu and that the only way to resolve the impasse through a negotiated settlement was to engage with Etete and Malabu, whether we liked it or not.' As Etete and Malabu's ownership of OPL 245 was disputed, to say the least, this left Shell in a tricky position. The implication was that any payment for OPL 245 involving Malabu was by definition improper.

Shell's and especially ENI's claims of innocence became harder to maintain in September 2019 when, under oath in a Milan courtroom, a Shell executive vice-president, Ian Craig, maintained that ENI's chief executive had met privately with Nigeria's president, Goodluck Jonathan, shortly before the OPL 245 deal was sealed. Goodluck Jonathan was both an old political friend of Dan Etete and, as the former governor of the oil-rich Nigerian state of Bayelsa, well acquainted with senior oil company executives. The ideal middleman, in fact.

At the time of writing, investigations into corruption and collusion regarding the OPL 245 sale are ongoing, but with each revelation by the Dutch, Italian and Nigerian investigating teams the original Shell and ENI line of 'we bought the assets in good faith' appears increasingly tenuous. As for Dan Etete, in 2016 Nigeria's Economic and Financial Crime Commission (EFCC) charged him with money laundering over the OPL 245 sale. This relates to the accusation that the US$1.3 billion Shell and ENI paid to the Nigerian government via Goodluck Jonathan was then moved on to Etete, who redistributed approximately one third of it back to Jonathan and other senior Nigerian government officials in the form of bribes, emoluments and kickbacks to see the OPL 245 deal through. Etete, living in exile in Dubai, denied the EFCC's findings. In fact, Etete, Shell, ENI and Goodluck Jonathan deny all accusations of wrongdoing levelled at them.

In an interesting aside to the affair, the OPL 245 sale was concluded just months after Shell had paid a US$30 million settlement against previous allegations of bribery in Nigeria and elsewhere. It meant that Shell needed to watch its step as it was now effectively on probation. It conducted a large proportion of its business in America and, following its hefty bribery settlement, had been forced to give assurances to the US Department of Justice that its operations were all above board.

SOUTH AFRICA

The end of apartheid in South Africa in 1994 was supposed to herald a new era of equality, opportunity and inclusion in the newly liberated 'rainbow nation'. So how did it come about that in 2019 the World Bank declared South Africa to be the most unequal nation on Earth? The short answer is corruption, made possible by South Africa being to all intents and purposes a one-party state ruled exclusively since 1994 by the African National Congress (ANC).

In recent years, the presidency of Jacob Zuma in 2009–2018 has been seen as the high-water mark of state-sponsored corruption. When Zuma was forced to resign in 2018, the Judicial Commission of Inquiry into Allegations of State Capture was established to dissect the illegalities of his time in office. The Zondo Commission, as the public inquiry is usually called, highlighted two large-scale corruption cases with major deep-state entanglements. The first case centres around the logistics company Bosasa; the second concerns one of South Africa's richest and most powerful families, the Guptas.

The Bosasa bonanza

Bosasa was owned by Gavin Watson, a white former rugby star who, along with his three brothers, found fame in 1976 when they began playing in black-only teams and then joined the ANC. In short, he was one of the good guys.

As prominent opponents of a racist regime, the Watsons thrived after the end of apartheid in 1994. They ran several businesses and acted as mentors and trainers for a rising class of black businesspeople and entrepreneurs for a government eager to promote a positive discrimination policy known as Black Economic Empowerment (BEE). Gavin Watson's company Bosasa, which he acquired in 2000, did especially well out of BEE, hiring predominantly black employees and then calling in favours from his former ANC colleagues now in government to land lucrative work contracts. Where appealing to the political consciousness of his anti-apartheid compadres failed, Watson turned to corruption instead and handed out generous bribes worth US\$5 million to ANC government officials up to and including, it is alleged, President Jacob Zuma, who had come to power in 2009.

This is what put Watson's activities over and above the everyday corruption that is endemic to South African life. By using the political capital he had built up during apartheid, Gavin Watson activated a network of bureaucratic contacts and political placemen to do his bidding and further his interests against those of the South African people. When questions were asked why Bosasa was quite so popular among government purchasing departments, Watson simply told Zuma to call off the dogs or else he would deny him further access to 'Gavin's Safe', the vault in his company office that was specially set aside to contain bribe money.

At least, that was the story told by ex-Bosasa senior executive Angelo Agrizzi to the Zondo Commission in autumn 2019. Agrizzi revealed that Watson called his slush fund 'monopoly money', not because there was so much of it but because he intended to use it to 'get the monopoly of state business'. In a dramatic courtroom twist, Agrizzi also testified that one of Bosasa's compliant officials was Khotso De Wee, the secretary of the Zondo Commission itself. De Wee denied the allegations but was nevertheless removed from the inquiry. Other supposed Watson moles included the deputy director of public prosecutions and the head of a special unit set up to investigate Bosasa, both of whom were fired.

Another alleged collaborator in Gavin Watson's deep state was Linda Mti, an old ANC ally from the apartheid era. Was it at Watson's instigation that Jacob Zuma while South Africa's deputy president made Mti prisons commissioner in 2001? If not, it was a remarkable piece of serendipity that a Watson family friend was now in charge of a department in which Bosasa had a special interest. Bosasa ran two government detention centres when Mti took his ministerial seat; within a matter of months the company had won the very profitable catering contracts for all of the country's prisons and their 160,000 inmates. Mti also unwittingly played a starring role in a secretly recorded audio made in 2016, when Gavin Watson was heard coaching him in advance of a meeting with President Zuma regarding an investigation into Bosasa. 'Now Mr President, you need to close this thing,' Watson instructed Mti to say. Watson also went on to brag that he would get Zuma to appoint someone to South Africa's National Prosecuting Authority who was susceptible to his control. 'We need the right person in the right place,' he said.

The picture that emerged from the ongoing Zondo Commission is of a nation where apartheid-era networks of ANC solidarity and support have been transformed in the post-apartheid era into extra-legal networks of economic extortion and political subversion. With allegations of wrongdoing swirling around it, Bosasa rebranded as African Global Operations in 2016, but the revelations of the Zondo Commission meant the company lost most of its business and went into liquidation. Gavin Watson himself was unable to appear at the Zondo Commission, as the 71-year-old died in a car crash in August 2019, possibly while trying to flee the country.

A family affair

South Africa is a big country with room for more than one deep state. In fact, the crimes of Gavin Watson were small beer compared to the state-threatening activities of the Gupta brothers. The family's alleged crimes are numerous, and were laid bare by repeated witness testimonies at the Zondo Commission, as we'll see below.

Atul, Ajay and Rajesh Gupta relocated to South Africa from the north Indian state of Uttar Pradesh in 1993, just as the country was emerging from apartheid and a new, inexperienced political class was attempting to remake the nation. The Guptas, with Ajay as their driving force, thrived in the new South Africa, building up a computer sales business then branching out into mining, aerospace, the media and other industries. They hit on a winning formula of courting South Africa's elites by throwing lavish parties at their opulent Saxonworld estate near Johannesburg. Celebrities, sports stars and politicians were all regular Gupta guests, none more so than Jacob Zuma, who was South Africa's deputy president when he first met the family in 2002.

Demonstrators protest against the overweening power of the Guptas, their banner showing president Jacob Zuma literally in the family's pocket.

Zuma was one of the country's most controversial politicians. Outspoken and not averse to testing the boundaries of the law, he was dismissed in 2005 after being implicated in a bribery case involving a South African Indian businessman, Schabir Shaik. By this time, the Guptas were already aware of Zuma's alleged bribe-taking tendencies and they had done their first kindness for him in 2003, when they hired Zuma's son, Duduzane. Although he was technically an employee, the Guptas treated Duduzane like one of the family. They gave him repeated promotions and bought property for him, including a US$1.3 million apartment in Dubai's Burj Khalifa, the world's tallest skyscraper.

When Jacob Zuma became president of South Africa in 2009, the Guptas wanted a return on their investment. The first thing they needed help with was financing the launch of their newspaper, *The New Age*, in 2010. The media minister, Themba Maseko, was summoned to see the Guptas and told to sign over to them the entire state media advertising budget of US$80 million. Maseko refused and was told by Ajay Gupta that he would 'speak to my seniors in government, who would sort me out and replace me with people who would cooperate with him'. Maseko held firm, and a few months later was sacked. Maseko's successor proved more amenable, and the advertising budget was duly transferred.

In October 2010, the Guptas initiated another deep-state operation to bend government policy to their advantage. This time, Ajay Gupta told junior ANC member of parliament Vyjtie Mentor that he would see her appointed as minister of public enterprise if she pushed through policies that benefited Gupta aerospace interests. Mentor agreed and took the job, but after having second thoughts a few days later she was unceremoniously sacked.

This same pattern was played out when the Guptas wanted to open their own TV news station, ANN7. The media minister, Lulama Mokhobo, was ordered to come to Saxonworld and told to issue the relevant licence. When ANN7 began broadcasting in 2013 it was described by one of its journalists as a 'mafia station' pumping out Gupta-approved propaganda. Duduzane Zuma was on the channel's board of directors, and Rajesh Sundarem, the station's inaugural editor, revealed that Jacob Zuma regularly attended editorial meetings to ensure the proposed news bulletins were sufficiently pro-government. Ultimately, though, ANN7 was all about the Guptas and Sundarem was told to merely humour both Zumas and then disregard their input.

To burnish the Guptas' reputation further, the prestigious London-based PR firm Bell Pottinger was retained at great expense. This backfired badly when Bell Pottinger oversaw a hugely controversial social media campaign implying that any criticism of, or investigation into, the Guptas was a racially motivated dirty tricks campaign orchestrated by 'white monopoly capital' to impose 'economic apartheid' on South Africa. At the same time the accounting giant KPMG was hired to rebut the findings of one such investigation by state tax authorities. This they duly did in a report that labelled the Guptas' auditors a 'rogue unit'. The ploy worked, with several senior tax officials forced to resign.

Eventually, though, the family's bluff was called. They were keen to complete a deal for a uranium mine they had tried to buy in 2010 (with government money supplied by Zuma) in order to cash in on the opening of Russian-built nuclear power stations in South Africa. For years the proposed mine purchase and the power station contracts had been the subjects of official investigations – and rightly so, as Jacob Zuma had specified as part of the deal to the Russians that the uranium fuel for their power plants could only be supplied by the Guptas' mine. By 2015 the Guptas were keen to end the stalemate. Using his tried and tested government jobs-for-favours tactic, Ajay Gupta promised to promote South Africa's deputy finance minister Mcebisi Jonas if he sacked treasury officials who were still asking awkward questions about the Russia-uranium deal. When Jonas pointed out that Gupta, as a private citizen, had no authority to make government appointments, Ajay Gupta told him: 'You must understand that we are in control of everything. [Zuma] will do anything we tell him to do.' The deep state had, momentarily, come to the surface.

Jonas refused Gupta's offer and, daringly, with so much at stake, outed Ajay Gupta in public in March 2016. Coming from a senior ANC government official, Jonas' accusation was hard to dismiss and action needed to be taken. Rattled by having their bluff called, the Guptas fled to Dubai, where they remain at the time of writing.

The fallout spread far and wide as other examples of Gupta wrongdoing emerged. Executives at McKinsey and KPMG lost their jobs over work they did with the family, while KPMG was also officially investigated for its Gupta links, as were HSBC and Standard Chartered. Bell Pottinger, meanwhile, went bust. Jacob Zuma was forced out of office in February 2018, protesting his innocence, and Duduzane Zuma was arrested on corruption charges a few months later. The era of the 'Zuptas', the Zumas and the Guptas, was over.

The end result of the Guptas' activities has been the financial evisceration of South Africa. Today, the country has the worst income inequality in the world. By citing a racial motive for the investigations against them, the Guptas also reopened a wound that the ending of apartheid was designed to heal. Many white South Africans point to the endemic corruption as the fault of mainly black ANC government mismanagement, while Indian South Africans find themselves seen as somehow culpable for the Guptas' actions. Black South Africans, meanwhile, remain desperately poor.

ZIMBABWE

With sizeable deposits of coal and iron ore, as well as platinum, gold and diamonds, Zimbabwe should be a wealthy country. Yet 74 per cent of Zimbabweans live in poverty, existing on less than US$5.50 a day and, according to the country's largest trade union, the unemployment rate is as high as 90 per cent. There is corruption, of course, among the political class and the armed forces especially, but behind the everyday illegalities, payoffs and spoils of office there's an organized deep state at work. It is carefully and methodically permeating the country, influencing events from afar and supporting a regime that many others are reluctant to be associated with. Zimbabwe's deep state is China.

Investors from the east

China has been courting resource-rich and cash-poor nations in Africa since the 1990s, buying influence through major investments, large-scale infrastructure projects and business development. But its relationship with Zimbabwe goes back even further, and is inextricably linked with the fortunes of the country's ruling ZANU-PF Party.

Zimbabwe has existed as an independent nation since 1980. It emerged out of the former British colony of Southern Rhodesia following a 16-year conflict between a white minority government and two black majority independence parties, the socialist Zimbabwe African People's Union (ZAPU), supported by the Soviet Union, and the China-backed Zimbabwe African National Union – Patriotic Front (ZANU–PF).

With Robert Mugabe's ZANU–PF in charge, China continued its association with the new nation of Zimbabwe. China was fully aware of Zimbabwe's abundant natural resources and economic potential and was prepared to play the long game, supporting Mugabe across the many controversies of his 36-year regime. Throughout the 1980s and 1990s China poured money into Zimbabwean mining, agriculture, energy and construction. By the 2010s it was Zimbabwe's main export market and was the largest foreign investor in the country. In 2015, the state-owned Power Construction Corporation of China sealed a US$1.2 billion deal to revamp Zimbabwe's largest thermal power plant, while China's Sinohydro Group secured a contract worth US$335 million to expand another major power station. Zimbabwe also awarded a trio of solar power projects to Chinese companies that same year.

Diamonds are forever

China's generosity was always tempered by its opposition to Mugabe's 2008 'Indigenization' law that required foreign businesses in the country to be 51 per cent owned by Zimbabweans. It was a piece of legislation that China never liked and always wanted repealed. And, for one key industry, it was a wish shared by Zimbabwe's army. Diamonds were big business in Zimbabwe, and Chinese companies such as Anjin Investment and Jinan Mining were key players in it – as were Zimbabwe's armed forces, which operated a kind of protection racket over the diamond trade. While the Chinese and the army undoubtedly did very well out of diamonds, the repeal of the Indigenization law would have given them even greater access to the highly lucrative enterprise in a co-dependent relationship: the Chinese required Zimbabwean army support and security to widen its diamond-mining interests; the army needed China's connections and access to wider international markets to maximize the profits it received from its share in the diamond trade.

So long as Mugabe maintained his tight grip on power, both China and the army had to endure the privations of not controlling 100 per cent of Zimbabwe's diamond market. Then, in 2017, their luck changed when Mugabe fell out with, and ordered the arrest of, his deputy and heir-apparent, Emmerson Mnangagwa, who quickly went into exile. Suddenly, China was presented with a potential ZANU–PF leader it could deal with and a disaffected army ready to act, which it duly did on 14 November 2017 when the 93-year-old Mugabe was ousted in a military coup. He was replaced by Mnangagwa, who went on to assume full presidential powers when he won a disputed and probably rigged election the following year. Although independent observers and many overseas states questioned the result, China declared the election 'peaceful and orderly' and called on the world to respect 'the choice made by the people of Zimbabwe'.

So, was China complicit in the coup? If it was, like any competent deep state it hid the evidence well. It certainly had the means, motive and opportunity. A series of convenient coincidences also point to illicit Chinese involvement. For example, Mnangagwa, while on the run from Mugabe's police, paid a visit to Beijing just weeks before the coup. Was he there to seek Chinese support to usurp Mugabe, Zimbabwe-watchers asked? The speculation increased further when it was revealed that the coup's instigator, General Constantino Chiwenga, had been in China just days before the military takeover. It was described as a routine visit, but the timing is suspicious, to say the least.

Emmerson Mnangagwa delivers his inauguration speech as provisional president in Harare, December 2017, shortly after replacing his former mentor, Robert Mugabe.

What is clear is that since Mugabe's fall Zimbabwe-China relations have improved, and they only got better after Chiwenga was appointed vice-president in late 2017 and then reached all all-time high when President Mnangagwa repealed the troublesome Indigenization law in August 2019.

CHAPTER 6

CENTRAL AND SOUTH AMERICA

THIS REGION'S HISTORY has been shaped by the blessing and the curse of its natural resources. Since the first Europeans arrived in the late 1400s the continent has been viewed as a vast source of plunder, with the largest or most ruthless exploiters benefiting most from its precious metals, minerals, rubber, agricultural produce and oil. It's an attitude that continues today, creating a climate where corporate power trumps people power, where authoritarian leadership has deeper roots than democracy, and where the strategic needs of the superpower neighbour to the north has a pervasive influence. In more recent times, it has allowed drug syndicates to amass unimaginable wealth, infiltrating governments and turning several regional powers into 'narco-states'.

In short, Central and South America is the perfect arena in which deep states flourish. This chapter examines some of the most infamous examples of the deep state at work in this complex and often troubled region.

CORPORATE DEEP STATES

Capitalism and corruption are old friends. This is especially true where there are great inequalities of wealth between the haves and the have-nots, as there are in Latin America. The continent's recent history is littered with examples of commercial enterprises buying their way to power and influence in the face of compromised or unstable regimes. We can legitimately call these 'corporate deep states'.

Some operate openly, sponsoring violence and revolution, as United Fruit did in Guatemala in the 1950s; others adopt a more cloak-and-dagger approach, for example ITT during the Chile coup of 1973. Finally, there are those that take the parliamentary road to conspiracy, as in Brazil, whose powerful agribusinesses have infiltrated that country's parliament and dictate whole areas of government policy.

It's worth exploring each of these three examples, to really understand the different ways in which corporate deep states work.

UNITED FRUIT GUATEMALA COUP

United Fruit was founded in 1899 by Minor Cooper Keith. The native New Yorker had been helping to develop Costa Rica's railway network when, as a speculative business idea, he began growing bananas to supply the market for them in the USA. He found himself swamped with orders and, needing more land to meet the growing demand, he cleverly cut deals with newly emerging states including Honduras, Panama and Colombia to build their railway networks in return for huge tracts of plantation land. Jamaica, Cuba and the Dominican Republic also fell under the company's sway. Business boomed.

By the early 20th century United Fruit had outgrown Costa Rica. It was now El Pulpo ('the Octopus'), a multinational whose tentacles reached into all aspects of Central American life. It ignored local labour laws, paid little or no taxes, ran a network of workplace spies and enforcers, and generated an economy larger than many of its host countries: in 1930, for example, United Fruit was worth US$215 million; by contrast, the GDP of Nicaragua, where United Fruit had extensive interests, was US$127 million.

At its peak, United Fruit employed 67,000 people and controlled millions of acres of land, most of it held in reserve – to the displeasure of local peasants who were therefore unable to farm it. To move its product, the company operated 2,400 km (1,490 miles) of railroad and commanded a private navy, the Great White Fleet, at one point the biggest shipping line in the world. To ensure the smooth running of its banana-based empire, United Fruit also adopted a policy of bribery and coercion among local officials and national politicians throughout Central America.

United Fruit won powerful friends in the United States, too. Basing itself in Boston, Massachusetts, it acquired investors and board members from among the city's most influential families, known as the Boston Brahmins, a tight-knit group that provided many of the country's senior politicians, industrialists and civil servants: the Cabot Lodges, Peabodys, Lowells, and Jefferson Coolidges. This was America's WASP elite – white Anglo-Saxon Protestant patricians at the centre of political, social and economic life.

Birth of the banana republic

Well-connected in the United States and all-powerful in Central America, United Fruit became a law unto itself. In 1910 a workers' protest on a company plantation in Guatemala was ended by paid enforcers lynching its ringleader, followed by the lynching party boss being hired as superintendent on one of the farms. Worse still, when United Fruit workers at a company plant in Ciénaga,

Colombia, went on strike in 1928 for better pay and conditions, government troops, with company approval, opened fire on a workers' mass meeting. Up to 2,000 protesters died.

Such was the company's association with shady Latin American politics that, in 1904, the American writer O. Henry used it as the

The magnificent entrance to a United Fruit Company building in New Orleans.

model for 'Vesuvius Fruit', the rapacious company that corrupts the fictitious country of Anchuria in his novel *Cabbages and Kings*. Henry also coined the phrase 'banana republic' in his book, and it proved prophetic. In 1911 United Fruit looked on approvingly as another fruit magnate, Sam Zemurray, engineered a coup against the president of Honduras after he introduced a land reform bill Zemurray disagreed with. After removing the democratically elected head of state, Zemurray replaced him with his own proxy, former president Manuel Bonilla. As a sign of his gratitude, Bonilla reversed his predecessor's reforms, awarded Zemurray 35,000 hectares (86,480 acres) of land, exempted him from paying tax and, in an audacious act of deep-state duplicity, allowed Zemurray to invoice Honduras for the then-astronomical sum of US$500,000 to cover the costs he had incurred in staging the coup.

In 1954, United Fruit dusted down the playbook Zemurray had written when it faced its own land dispute with the government of Guatemala. The company owned around 40 per cent of Guatemala's agricultural land, so alarm bells sounded when the country's left-wing populist president, Jacobo Árbenz, proposed compulsorily purchasing much of that acreage to give to the country's landless peasants. United Fruit did not use much of that land anyway, but that was beside the point. Its hegemony was being threatened and it needed to act.

At the same time, the United States was in the grip of a 'red scare', with both the House Un-American Activities Committee (HUAC) and Senator Joseph McCarthy conducting public hearings aimed at unmasking public and political figures with supposed communist sympathies. In the summer of 1953 Soviet spies Julius and Ethel Rosenberg had sensationally been executed for treason after a much-publicized trial. On 12 August 1953 the USSR successfully tested its first hydrogen bomb. All of this appeared to be a fulfilment of former US secretary of defense James Forrestal's prediction in 1949 that 'the Russian's are coming'. Yes, said United Fruit, and they're coming to Guatemala.

Guatemala's former president Jacobo Árbenz and his wife in 1955, the year after his deposition.

United Fruit's anti-Árbenz campaign was made easier by John Forster Dulles, the US secretary of state, and his brother Allen Dulles, head of the CIA. Both men had once been legal advisors to United Fruit and retained links to – and shares in – the business. Meanwhile, at the United Nations, America's ambassador Henry Cabot Lodge successfully lobbied against Árbenz. A pure-bred Boston Brahmin, Cabot Lodge was also a United Fruit stockholder and, while serving in the US Senate, had publicly championed the company. Finally, for die-hard conspiracy theorists, President Eisenhower's personal secretary, Anne Whitman, was married to United Fruit's public relations director.

By 1954 United Fruit had been busily undermining Jacobo Árbenz for a while. After he was elected in 1951 the company had begun organizing 'fact-finding' missions to Guatemala, feeding friendly journalists stories of Árbenz's plans to turn the country into a Soviet-style workers' paradise. Meanwhile, the fervently anti-communist journalist John Clements was hired to concoct the 235-page and largely fictitious *Report on Guatemala*, which detailed Marxist infiltration into Guatemala's government and claimed that Árbenz intended to seize the strategically important Panama Canal. A copy of the *Report* was sent to every member of the US Congress and to a select group of national opinion-formers.

In parallel, the United States Information Agency (USIA), an official government body, produced a *Chronology of Communism in Guatemala* pamphlet and published three anti-Árbenz documentaries for broadcast across Latin America. The CIA joined in by setting up *La Voz de la Liberacion* ('the Voice of Liberation'), a radio station that encouraged the people of Guatemala to rise up and overthrow their president.

In the event, ordinary Guatemalans didn't need to overthrow anybody. United Fruit and the CIA did it for them. The pretext for the removal of Árbenz was the price he paid United Fruit for their expropriated land. Although it was a generous US$2.86 an acre (United Fruit had paid US$1.48), United Fruit claimed the land was worth US$75 an acre. As Árbenz reclaimed some 386,901 acres, this meant a shortfall of almost US$30 million. The company duly submitted an invoice for this amount to the Guatemalan government, accompanied by a menacing US State Department letter claiming that Árbenz's valuation did not bear 'the slightest resemblance to just evaluation'. When Árbenz refused to pay, United Fruit and the CIA activated Operation Success, the coup to topple Guatemala's government, on 18 June 1954.

Just nine days later Árbenz had been deposed by a coalition of disaffected exiles, CIA operatives, paid mercenaries and complicit elements of the Guatemalan army. Árbenz's replacement, Colonel Carlos Castillo Armas, lasted barely a year before being assassinated. By 1960 Guatemala had descended into a 30-year civil war that left 200,000 people dead and a quarter of a million displaced. Undeterred, United Fruit went on to enjoy a 90 per cent share of the Guatemalan banana market for the rest of the century. Needless to say, Árbenz's land reforms were quietly shelved.

New brands, old habits

By the 1970s United Fruit had merged with another food company, AMK, to become the United Brands Company. Yet despite the new name, old habits died hard. In 1974, United Brands' chief executive Eli Black was caught bribing the president of Honduras, Oswaldo López Arellano. Black responded by throwing himself from the 44th floor of the Pan-Am Building in New York City, while Arellano was ousted in a military coup. It was just like old times.

In the early 1980s the company changed hands once more, rebranding itself as Chiquita. It hit the headlines again in 2007, when Chiquita was slapped with a US$25 million US Justice Department fine after admitting paying protection money in Colombia to the AUC, an outlawed right-wing paramilitary group linked to the country's cocaine cartels. In a neat piece of historical symmetry harking back to the glory days of the Dulles brothers, the deal between Chiquita and the US Justice Department was brokered by the company's high-powered lawyer Eric Holder, who went on to serve as Barack Obama's attorney-general in 2009–15.

Chiquita's Justice Department fine was followed in 2016 by a wrongful death lawsuit launched by the families of five Christian missionaries and a geologist murdered by another outlawed Colombian paramilitary group, FARC, that had been paid protection money by Chiquita. At the same time, Colombia's attorney-general also issued charges against 13 Chiquita executives for its links to FARC.

CHILE: THE ITT COUP

Unlike Guatemala, Chile was not a corruption-plagued banana republic. Stretching 4,270 km (2,653 miles) along the high line of the Andes, Chile has a climate that was reflected in its national character – cool and temperate. Until 65-year-old Salvador Allende came to power in 1970, that is.

An avowed Marxist, like many South American leaders Allende was a critic of vast corporations and foreign powers stripping his country's assets and exporting capital overseas in what he called a 'doctrine of excess profits'. His plan for Chile involved nationalizing several key industries in order to reclaim some of its wealth.

Of all the multinationals operating in Chile, including PepsiCo, Ford and Chase Manhattan Bank, telecoms giant the International Telephone & Telegraph Corporation (ITT) led the resistance. They began their 'stop Allende' campaign before the 1970 election. John McCone, an ITT senior executive, had also been director of the CIA in 1961–65, and he opened a line of contact between his new employer and his old one. In a later US congressional hearing into the coup, McCone revealed he had offered the USA US$1 million in ITT funds to use 'as it saw fit' against Allende.

When that failed and Allende won the election, President Richard Nixon gave his secret services US$7 million to facilitate Allende's removal. 'All's fair on Chile,' Nixon told his national security advisor, Henry Kissinger. 'Kick 'em in the ass. OK?' Nixon was particularly receptive to ITT's concerns as they were a client of his old law firm and he remained on good terms with their chairman and chief executive, Howard Geneen, and had wined and dined him on board the *Sequoia*, the presidential yacht. In return, ITT sponsored the 1972 Republican National Convention to the tune of US$400,000. The company may well have expected a quid pro quo from Nixon when Allende turned his attention to ITT after nationalizing Chile's copper and nitrate mines, which were operated by the American-owned Anaconda and Kennecott groups.

A classic move

The Chilean Telephone Company (CHITELCO) was a prize ITT asset, generating annual profits of US$60 million. When discussions began on transferring its ownership to the state they immediately hit a stumbling block. As with United Fruit's land in Guatemala, the two parties could not agree a valuation. ITT said CHITELCO was worth US$153 million; the government offered US$24 million. Deciding that further negotiation was pointless, ITT ramped up the secret campaign to remove Allende's regime.

Testifying before the same post-coup committee as John McCone, senior ITT vice-president Edward J. Gerrity detailed how he and CIA agents used President Nixon's US$7 million slush fund to pay agitators to foment debilitating strikes and industrial unrest among the nation's truckers, taxi drivers and shopkeepers that eroded support for Allende's regime. It was a classic deep state move: whip up popular unrest, then cite that unrest as your reason to ride to the rescue in support of the 'will of the people'. Apart from funding strikes, ITT also poured cash into *El Mercurio*, a right-wing Chilean newspaper whose thunderous editorials against Allende helped to create a climate of fear and loathing against him.

Codenamed Operation Fubelt, the coup when it came was swift. It began at 7.00 am on 11 September 1973, with coordinated rebel naval, air force and army action against strategic positions. Radio and TV networks were closed and the presidential palace, with Allende inside, was attacked. By 2.30 pm the government had fallen and Allende was dead. The circumstances are not clear, but the consensus is that he shot himself with an AK-47 rifle given to him by Fidel Castro.

General Augusto Pinochet emerged from the putsch as Chile's new leader. For the next 17 years he ruled as a military dictator, cracking down on dissent, allowing exploitative businesses to operate with impunity, lining his pockets and keeping in America's good books. At least 3,000 people were killed under Pinochet's rule, and almost 30,000 Chileans experienced state-administered torture. As for the companies whose assets had been expropriated, such as Anaconda, Kennecott and ITT, Pinochet compensated them all in full.

The Presidential Palace in Chile burns during the CIA- and ITT-funded coup of 1973.

BANCADA IN BRAZIL

Brazil's modern history is one of short periods of democracy interspersed with coups, military dictatorships and civil unrest. This instability has left the country vulnerable to both 'everyday' political corruption and to more pervasive manipulation at the hands of powerful interest groups.

Not the least of these is a cartel of giant mining concerns and international agribusinesses known as the *bancada ruralista*. It funds around 40 per cent of Brazil's politicians, sending them off to the country's National Congress in Brasília to represent its interests through a caucus called the Parliamentary Agricultural and Livestock Front. More than a lobby group, the *bancada ruralista* is a deep-state enclave in the heart of Brazil's parliament. It protects its interests politically in two main ways: by placing its representatives in key government posts and by the systematic corruption of state officials.

An example of the first approach is the appointment of Blairo Maggi as minister of agriculture during the presidency of Michel Temer in 2016–18. Maggi was the billionaire owner of the Amaggi Group, the world's largest soy bean producer and, courtesy of Greenpeace, the 2006 recipient of the Golden Chainsaw award for his contribution to the desecration of Brazil's rainforest in the pursuit of ever-more land on which to plant his crops. Brazil grows one-third of the world's soy beans, exporting most of them to China, and the crop accounts for almost a quarter of the country's GDP. Maggi's elevation to the strategic agriculture post was therefore no coincidence; he was put there to protect and further his and his fellow agribusiness colleagues' interests. Even when Maggi was replaced in 2019 it was simply a like-for-like transfer, the new minister being Tereza Cristina Dias, previously leader of the *bancada* caucus in parliament.

Blairo Maggi was appointed as minister of agriculture in 2016, where he could protect his company's interests from regulation.

As for the deep state corrupting its way to power, the activities of the meat-processing behemoth JBS are archetypal. JBS slaughters 13 million animals every day and generates annual revenues of US$50 billion. Everything it does is on a grand scale, including its malfeasance. In 2017 JBS received one of the biggest fines in global corporate history – US$3.2 billion – after admitting bribing more than 1,800 politicians over a number of years to the tune of US$250 million. 'It was the rule of the game . . . Corruption was on the upper floor, with the authorities,' said Joesley Batista, JBS' co-owner. He admitted this after secretly taped conversations came to light in which he and then-president Michel Temer discussed who and how much to bribe across various government positions.

Bolsonaro in power

For one brief moment in early 2019, many Brazilians thought that things were changing. This was after they elected as president Jair Bolsonaro, a maverick and unpredictable political outsider in the Donald Trump mould.

Like Trump, Bolsonaro was a protectionist, an advocate of trade tariffs and a 'my country first' approach to business. At least, he was until he took office. Just weeks into his administration, Bolsonaro unaccountably became a born-again economic liberal, embracing free trade, corporate tax cuts and the privatization of the state-owned oil and utilities companies, Petrobras and Eletrobras, as well as the state bank, Banco do Brasil. While this completely contradicted Bolsonaro's old beliefs, it chimed perfectly with the wishes of the *bancada ruralista* and their business partners in the USA such as the giant food-processing and shipping corporations Cargill, Bunge and ADM.

Proof that Jair Bolsonaro was firmly in the *bancada* camp came in August 2019, when the annual 'burning season' began in the rainforest. Every summer, Brazil's farmers and agribusinesses are allowed to slash and burn a strictly defined area of the forest in order to clear land for grazing and crop growth. Each year they

A demonstration in support of Operação Lava Jato in São Paulo, 2015. The ambitious anti-corruption effort found itself thwarted by the deep state time and again.

flagrantly exceed their burning quota, usually with little or no punishment. But in 2019, under Bolsonaro's watch, the abuse was the worst it had been for 10 years. Just under 90,000 fires were recorded, a 30 per cent increase on the number of blazes from the previous year. An area of 906,000 hectares (2.25 million acres) was destroyed, the deforested land turned over to the *bancada ruralistas* for soy bean planting, cattle grazing and mining use.

While the rest of the planet looks upon the Amazonian rainforest as 'the lungs of the world', for the *bancada ruralista* it's just fields that haven't been cleared yet. Despite professing 'profound love and respect' for the Amazon, it appeared that Bolsonaro agreed.

Operation car wash

A fascinating example of Brazil's deep state at its worst was the Operação Lava Jato ('Operation Car Wash') investigation that began in 2014. It centred on a massive fraud and bribery scandal run by executives of the state-owned oil conglomerate Petrobras. Up to US$2.5 billion was diverted from the company's coffers into a slush fund used to finance political campaigns and bribe politicians and officials. Eighteen companies were implicated in its findings and 429 individuals indicted, with 159 convicted.

Operation Car Wash was established under the presidency of Dilma Rousseff, whose Workers' Party had by 2014 ruled Brazil for 13 years. While Rousseff saw the probe as a means of addressing Brazil's corrupt political culture, the *bancada ruralista* saw it differently. For them – and this is where Operation Car Wash is elevated from an 'ordinary' corruption scandal into an audacious deep state takeover – it was an opportunity to destroy Rousseff and her party using the very investigation she had instigated.

Using all of the dark arts of lobbying, negative briefing, media attacks and the corruption of Operation Car Wash officials, the *bancada* portrayed the scandal as an almost wholly Workers' Party-focused affair – when in fact most of those being investigated were aligned with the *bancada*. The public bought the lie and Rousseff's approval ratings fell to a dismal 6 per cent. 'We have to stop this shit . . . We have to change the government to be able to stop this bleeding,' said Romero Jucá, a high-ranking opposition politician. This came during a covertly recorded call with the former president of Brazil's largest oil and gas transportation company. In the same conversation, Jucá revealed that he had also been plotting Rousseff's downfall with a cabal of supreme court justices and military commanders. When Rousseff was finally removed from office in August 2016 it was presented as an impeachment. In reality it was a coup.

With Rousseff gone, the next phase was to shut down Operation Car Wash. In order to do this, the *bancada* was willingly assisted by Michel Temer, the new interim president. His political faction, the Brazilian Democratic Movement Party (PMDB in its Portuguese acronym), had never led a government before, even though it was the country's largest party. It preferred instead to make and break coalitions, forming alliances with other parties when it suited its interests (Brazil's political system is based on proportional representation, meaning all of its governments are coalitions of one sort or another). The PMDB was itself a party of factions, including conservatives, social democrats, evangelical Christians, farmers and far-leftists. The only ideology uniting these groups was a desire to share in the patronage and bribes that are the common currency of Brazilian politics.

With this in mind, Temer and his PMDB government was only too willing to shut down the Car Wash investigation – especially as Temer himself had been implicated in Petrobras' corruption allegations, along with no fewer than seven members of his cabinet.

But before they could do that, there was one more obstacle to overcome. The Supreme Court judge overseeing the Car Wash investigations was Teori Zavascki. In a judicial system notorious for its corruptibility, Zavascki stood out for his indestructible honesty. The deep state knew he could not be bought off at any price. So, what to do?

On 19 January 2017 a Hawker Beechcroft aircraft crashed 240 km (150 miles) off the coast of Rio de Janeiro. All four people on board were killed. One of them was Teori Zavascki. Problem solved.

THE RISE OF THE NARCO-STATES

Estimates vary, but the United Nations Office on Drugs and Crime (UNODC) puts annual narcotics revenues at around US$320,000 million. That's around 5 per cent of global GDP. In 2009 around 210 million people regularly took drugs; by 2017 that number was 271 million, at least 76 million of whom are in North America. Drugs are big business, and they are only getting bigger.

In the West, narcotics such as cocaine, heroin and marijuana originate in Central and South American countries including Colombia, Venezuela and Mexico. All of these can be described as narco-states, where governments and civil societies have been significantly compromised by drug trafficking.

159

All narco-states use corruption and violence to achieve their aims, but also indulge in PR exercises where necessary. For example, drug cartels will hand out cash and food to the poor and needy, or provide healthcare and public security in deprived and crime-ridden areas. In rural areas the coca, poppy and marijuana plantations they own generate incomes and jobs. In this way the traffickers are seen as Robin Hood figures, supported – loved even – by the very people they exploit.

While other territories, such as Bolivia, Peru, Nicaragua and Panama, contain significant narco-criminal elements, it's the three listed on page 159 that truly demonstrate how narco-states work, and they are the states focused on here.

COLOMBIA

Colombia's reputation for criminality, drug-inspired terrorism and rampant corruption was sealed during the 1980s at the hands of Pablo Escobar's Medellín Cartel and its sometime-ally/sometime-enemy the Cali Cartel. Both criminal enterprises openly bought and sold public officials, or killed them. Pablo Escobar called this policy *plata o plomo* ('silver or lead') and, faced with the choice of taking a bribe or taking a bullet, most public officials chose the former. And there was plenty of cash to go around: at its 1980s height, the Medellín Cartel was making 15 tonnes of cocaine and turning over US$70 million *per day*; this at a time when junior judges were making just US$230 a month.

Such was Escobar's belief in his untouchability that he successfully ran for election to Colombia's parliament in 1982, a rare occurrence of the deep state surfacing in public. This allowed the drug kingpin to mix openly with his political affiliates. These included Alberto Santofimio Botero, a powerful Liberal Party grandee. In 2007 Santofimio was imprisoned for the assassination of two of his political rivals in the late 1980s. The murders were supposedly carried out by Escobar's men in return for services rendered by the former minister of justice.

A confident Pablo Escobar smiles for the camera in this 1976 police mug shot.

Apart from cultivating powerful politicians, Escobar was careful to keep the Catholic Church on side. He took to touring the slums of Medellín in the company of two local priests, Reverends Elías Lopera and Hernan Cuartas. They joined Escobar's charity foundation, Medellín Without Slums, and frequently appeared on platforms with him at public events. Lopera was a particular ally, and was portrayed as something of a saintly figure in the influential newspaper *Medellín Cívico* – whose owner was none other than Pablo Escobar.

By inveigling himself into the political and religious establishment, Escobar was playing a clever game, normalizing his image and burrowing deeper, and legitimately, into the heart of Colombia's establishment. However, this didn't last. When the Colombian government finally got tough on the drug cartels, Escobar showed his true colours. Following a 1984 raid on several of his jungle-based cocaine laboratories, Escobar murdered the minister of justice, Rodrigo Lara, effectively declaring war on the state. Escobar's brief spell as a public servant was over and he took the deep state back underground. The result was a conflict of almost unimaginable brutality and ongoing corruption and collusion. The government's attempts to defeat the cartels were constantly compromised by the traffickers receiving tip-offs on upcoming raids and arrests. In 1989, for example, the Medellín chief of police was sacked and the head of the national police resigned over their suspected links to the cartels.

By the early 1990s Colombia was the world's murder capital, with 25,100 deaths in 1991 and 27,100 in 1992. Yet when Escobar was killed in December 1993 by a special police unit, both the Medellín and Cali cartels were in decline, decimated by a series of drug seizures and high-profile arrests. During one raid on a Cali Cartel stronghold, Colombia's special forces found files containing the names of 2,800 politicians, journalists, congress members, state governors and military personnel on the traffickers' payroll. Despite these setbacks, the narco-criminals carried on corrupting. In 1994, for example, it was revealed that the newly elected president, Ernesto Samper, had accepted more than US$6 million in 'campaign contributions' from the Cali Cartel. Somehow, Samper remained in office.

This proved to be a last hurrah for the old way of doing things. As Colombia's government cracked down on corruption and criminality at the dawn of the new millennium, the traffickers did what any troubled corporation would do – they restructured and found new business partners.

Rebuilding

Phase one was rebuilding. By the end of the 1990s the Medellín and Cali Cartels had collapsed into around 300 smaller gangs known as *cartelitos* ('little cartels'). In time, they saw the benefits of working together and resurrected the old debt-collection arm of the Medellín Cartel, the Oficina de Envigado, and converted it into a federation of traffickers. Phase two was finding new states to infiltrate. While Colombia's cartels were busy reinventing themselves after Pablo Escobar's fall, Mexico's drug gangs took charge of the lucrative supply routes into the United States. The Colombians needed a new route to market that they could control, and they found it half a world away.

The West African nation of Guinea-Bissau is the world's fourth poorest country. Its police force is virtually non-existent and its political establishment is in disarray. Since achieving independence in 1973 it has experienced two coups and a civil war. No government lasts more than a few months. It is by any definition a failed state. Now, thanks to the Colombians, it is also a narco-state. The traffickers, having found in Guinea-Bissau a compliant and weakened partner, fly or ship their product in from South America, repackage it, then move it on to Europe and beyond.

These are good times for Colombia's traffickers. In 2017, they produced 1,400 tonnes of cocaine, the largest annual amount ever recorded. Also, by using the Guinea-Bissau connection the cocaine-colonialists don't have to pay high 'export taxes' to the Mexican cartels. They can offer smaller bribes to their African facilitators and avoid the many DEA (Drug Enforcement Agency) patrols in the borderlands between Latin America, the Caribbean and the USA.

This does not mean that Colombia's streets are safe again. Cocaine is still made there, generating the usual collateral damage of compromised officials and dead bodies. Between 2016 and 2018 almost 2,500 Colombian police officers were dismissed following allegations of corruption, and in 2017 Luis Gustavo Moreno Rivera, head of the country's anti-corruption unit, was himself arrested for accepting drug cartel bribes and money laundering. Based on Rivera's subsequent testimony, three Supreme Court justices and scores of legislators were also indicted.

On top of all this, Colombia's government is also engaged in a long-running conflict against Marxist revolutionary militias, particularly the Revolutionary Armed Forces of Colombia (or FARC, in its Spanish acronym), with which it has been at 'war' since 1964. FARC is deeply involved in cocaine trafficking, using narco-profits to buy weapons.

In 2017 FARC disbanded, handing over its weapons to UN inspectors, and reformed as a legal political party, the Common Alternative Revolutionary Force. While this was good news for Colombia's government there was a caveat. Not all of FARC's members agreed with the 2017 ceasefire and a splinter group continued the armed struggle – and the drug trafficking. Meanwhile, another guerrilla group, the Army of National Liberation (ELN), is still actively at war with the state and is also involved in the drugs-for-arms trade. Finally, in late 2019 another FARC faction announced it was resuming hostilities against the state.

This came at a time when an ambitious government programme to destroy Colombia's coca fields with pesticide sprays was revealed to have been an abject failure – so much so that it actually contrived to somehow increase crop yields.

With its coca reduction programme in tatters and America threatening to take away its lucrative drug-fighting subsidies (US$10 billion to date), Colombia's government has yet to formulate a new and viable plan to combat its rebel-led and Oficina da Envigado cocaine problems.

VENEZUELA

Cocaine is about more than money in Venezuela. It's a political weapon, too, a means for the state to strike back against its most implacable enemy, the USA. As such, Venezuela's narcotics industry has effectively been nationalized, turning the country into what some analysts call a 'mafia state'.

The tragedy is that none of this is necessary. Venezuela has the largest oil reserves in the world. Its 1.2 trillion barrels are enough to raise every Venezuelan out of the poverty that is endemic there. But there are two problems. First, it is heavy extra-crude oil, which is difficult to refine. Secondly, US sanctions against Venezuela's socialist government mean the country cannot secure the foreign investment or skilled workers it needs to properly run its oil plants and refineries. So, to replace the billions of missing petro-dollars Venezuela's leaders have invested instead in narco-dollars.

The Cartel of the Suns

An unholy alliance ensued as a result of the election of Hugo Chávez as Venezuela's president in 1998. A former army officer who had led a failed coup in 1992, Chávez held political views that were a populist blend of nationalism, Marxist rhetoric and anti-imperialism (which was interchangeable with anti-Americanism).

A few years before Chávez was elected, high-ranking rogue elements within Venezuela's armed forces, police, civil service and political class had involved themselves in the cocaine trade. They called themselves the Cartel of the Suns, the name originating in the gold star decorations worn on the epaulettes of Venezuela's National Guard. The cartel flourished around the time the USA imposed sanctions against Venezuela in an effort to end Chávez's left-wing regime. These sanctions drove the Cartel of the Suns into the arms of another of America's enemies, the revolutionary Islamic state of Iran. The cartel and Iran formed an alliance that involved moving cocaine, Hezbollah terrorists and dirty money around the world. They even had their own fleet of planes to do this, the Venezuelan-based Conviasa Airlines, which soon became known as 'Aeroterror'.

Hugo Chávez died in March 2013 and was succeeded by his deputy, Nicolás Maduro. Although Chávez left his country ravaged by food and water shortages, unemployment, poverty and discontent, he was canny and charismatic enough to gloss over these problems, blaming the USA for his people's woes. The famously dour Maduro was less able to excite popular support, and the discrepancies between ordinary Venezuelans' lives and those in the ruling class, particularly in the Cartel of the Suns, became more obvious than ever.

The president was widely believed to be controlled by Diosado Cabello, the leader of Venezuela's parliament and suspected commander of the Cartel of the Suns. In 2015 Cabello was publicly accused of drug trafficking by Venezuela's former chief of security, Leamsy Salazar, who had defected to the USA in 2014. Salazar also claimed the Cartel of the Suns worked with Cuba to move narcotics and laundered drug money through the state-owned oil company, PDVSA. Salazar's list of charges corroborates the similar testimony of Eladio Aponte, Venezuela's former supreme court chief, who had fled to the USA in 2012.

Venezuela's National Guard, which Diosado Cabello also controls, is particularly implicated in the Cartel of the Suns. In September 2013, officials at Paris' Charles de Gaulle Airport discovered 31 suitcases on board an Air France flight from Caracas, Venezuela, filled with 1.3 tonnes of cocaine worth US$220 million. Three National Guard officers based at Caracas Airport were later arrested in connection with the smuggling operation. The following

Nicolás Maduro (second left) at his presidential inauguration, accompanied – and watched over – by Diosado Cabello (centre).

year, a National Guard commander was apprehended while driving his family to the Venezuelan city of Valencia, his car loaded with 55 kg (1212 lb) of cocaine.

Keeping it in the family

Cabello and the National Guard don't have a monopoly on Venezuela's cocaine business. In November 2015, DEA agents arrested Efrain Antonio Campo Flores and Francisco Flores de Freitas, nephews of Cilia Flores, wife of Nicolás Maduro, for shipping 800 kg (1,764 lb) of cocaine from Haiti into the USA. Both men received 18 years' jail time in America. In addition, the First Lady of Venezuela's own son, a judge no less, is the subject of ongoing DEA investigations. Cilia Flores has also been linked to the case of Captain Yazenky Antonio Lamas Rondón, a pilot extradited to the US and accused of having made more than 100 narco-flights out of Venezuela.

The country's former vice-president, Tareck El Aissami, was sanctioned by the US in March 2019 for international drug trafficking. In July 2019 Hugo Carvajal Barrios, ex-head of the country's intelligence services, publicly stated that Maduro's government was involved in trafficking and corruption. He accused, among others, Néstor Reverol, former head of Venezuela's anti-drug trafficking agency – a man also under indictment by the US for drug-related corruption, with charges against him including blocking investigations and returning seized drugs to traffickers. Despite this, Reverol went on to serve as Venezuela's interior minister.

Venezuela's deep state is certainly an unusual one. It's as though many government officers arrange their working days on split schedules, attending to affairs of state (badly) before lunch, then administering the Cartel of the Suns (very profitably) in the afternoon. This means a kleptocracy in the upper echelons of the state enjoys unparalleled wealth while the people of Venezuela endure food and water shortages, power cuts, mass unemployment and almost comical levels of inflation.

MEXICO

There have been efforts by Mexican governments in recent decades to take on their country's drug cartels, but they have been largely botched operations that have only increased the power of the traffickers. This is partly because of the patronage and clientelism that are deeply ingrained in Mexican society and politics, going back to the colonial era of Spanish overlords dominating slave workers and indigenous populations. Large corporations, senior politicians and powerful drug cartels now act as modern-day overlords to lower-level clients, such as subordinate businesses, party politicians and government officials.

This can be seen in the case of the state-owned oil company Pemex, which in 2017 was sued by the Oro Negro oil-drilling company. Their lawsuit claimed that Oro Negro had been forced into bankruptcy for not paying Pemex the requisite bribes to secure lucrative government contracts. That same year, a much-trumpeted anti-corruption drive initiated by then-president Enrique Peña

Nieto was hamstrung when his own, presumably compromised, government refused to cooperate with the inquiry.

Narco criminals at large

The narco-criminality that plagues Mexican society today is more severe than it has ever been. As demand grew in the US for Mexican-made heroin after World War II, poppy farmers massively increased their operations. In the process they shared their profits with the country's dominant political party, the PRI, as a kind of tithe. Eventually, those individual farmers coalesced into a vast narco-industrial complex of powerful cartels. As they did, the balance of power changed, and what had once been an obligatory payment from subordinate farmers to their political masters switched to become a kind of gratuity bestowed by the dominant cartels on grateful and greedy state officials.

By the 1970s, Mexico's drug lords were mixing openly with the country's political leaders. At times, they even worked together against their common enemies. This was famously illustrated in the late 1970s and early 1980s, when major traffickers such as Miguel Ángel Félix Gallardo and Rafael Caro Quintero, with CIA assistance, helped to fund and train right-wing Nicaraguan Contra militias opposed to that country's democratically elected left-wing government.

Until the 1990s, the international narcotics market was dominated by Colombia's all-powerful Medellín and Cali cartels. When both went into decline in the later 1990s, Mexico's drug barons benefited most. As well as expanding the vast acreages given over to marijuana and poppy cultivation, Mexico's traffickers leveraged their geographical position between the drug vendors in Latin America and drug consumers in the USA to turn their borders into enormously profitable cocaine customs houses. International traffickers call it the 'trampoline', a quick bounce through Mexico being seen as an easier and quicker route into the USA than the DEA-infested waters of the Caribbean.

A rebel army fighting their country's left-wing Sandinista government, Nicaragua's right-wing Contras were generously funded by Mexico's drug lords – and later by America's National Security Agency (NSA).

La Linea

How Mexico's cartels influence the state is tried and tested, with regional officials, local police and army officers the first port of call when the traffickers arrive in town. One example is Ciudad Juárez, a particularly drug-saturated city that faces El Paso across the American border. It is controlled by the Juárez Cartel, whose armed enforcers are known as La Linea ('the Line'). This name derives from the unofficial line of demarcation between the cartel and the police. So long as the former keeps its activities within agreed limits of murder, mayhem, trafficking and general criminality, it can coexist quite happily with law enforcement officers. But La Linea is a physical border as well, one that applies all over Mexico. Major tourist areas are out of bounds for drug trafficking, for example, as are the enclaves of the rich and powerful. Everywhere else is up for grabs.

In some cases, this arrangement goes beyond coexistence and into collusion. Indeed, one of the most bloodthirsty cartels, the Zetas, grew out of a Mexican Special Forces military unit. In especially drug-infested areas such as Tijuana, close to the American border, police officers commonly moonlight as traffickers. One lowly patrolman who augmented his income like this in the early 1980s was Miguel Ángel Félix Gallardo, who went on to found the all-powerful Guadalajara Cartel.

Gallardo has been called the Henry Ford of trafficking, a true deep state innovator. His drug-manufacturing production line and distribution network was more streamlined, efficient and profitable than any established before or since. Central to his process was the bribing and, where necessary, punishment of state officials if they failed to sanction his activities or assist in the suppression of smaller, rival gangs. When Gallardo was jailed in 1989 for 37 years on a number of serious offences, several prominent police commanders were arrested too. Almost 100 police officers complicit in his criminal network simply vanished.

In December 2006, Mexico's new president Felipe de Jesús Calderón declared war on the cartels. Although some critics dismissed this as a stunt to divert attention from allegations of electoral fraud, Calderón pressed ahead with what he called his 'kingpin' strategy. This was a policy aimed at breaking up the big trafficking groups into smaller, less troublesome gangs. It was a huge mistake. Mexico's death rate, which had been falling, soared as a hellish drug war erupted. More than 275,000 people were killed over the next 13 years, most with no connection to the drugs trade. And it's not over yet: 2018 and 2019 recorded Mexico's highest murder rates in modern history, with 33,341 and 34,582 deaths respectively. This is what can happen when the actual state stands up to the deep state, and it's a big reason why it rarely does.

The result of this bloody carnage is that Mexico was left with scores of smaller narco-gangs, as anticipated, but was also still burdened with two huge cartels: the Sinaloa (which grew out of the Guadalajara Cartel) and the CJNG (Cártel de Jalisco Nueva Generación, or Jalisco New Generation Cartel). Both cartels, utterly ruthless and with huge armouries, are at war with each other, with most of the smaller drug gangs, and with the state.

Corruption wins again

One reason for the failure of Calderón's war on the cartels was corruption. Just how compromised Mexico's organs of state were was revealed at the sensational trial of Joaquín Guzmán in 2019.

Known as El Chapo ('Shorty') because of his diminutive size, Guzmán was a protégé of Félix Gallardo before becoming head of the Sinaloa Cartel. As he was the largest narco-celebrity since Pablo Escobar, Guzmán's arrest in 2016 and extradition to the USA for trial was a major coup for the DEA, and a major worry for many of Mexico's compromised elites.

Witness after witness lined up to deliver devastating revelations about state involvement in the drug trade. Vicente 'El Vincentello' Zambada Niebla, a high-ranking Sinaloa Cartel operative, told how Guzmán's organization spent US$1 million a month on bribes. Another witness outed former army general Gilberto Toledano as a prominent bribe-taker, pocketing payoffs of up to US$100,000 to allow drugs to pass through his district. Prison guards, police officers, lawyers, tax officials, airport workers and military personnel were all implicated in other evidence.

In one of the trial's biggest revelations, Genaro García Luna, Mexico's former public security director and the man overseeing the war on the cartels, was said by Vincente Zambada Niebla to have accepted multiple bribes, including one of US$56 million. Unfortunately, Héctor Beltrán Leyva, the former Sinaloa Cartel associate said to have made the payment, could not corroborate Niebla's story as he died of a heart attack in his prison cell the night before he was due to appear in court.

The Genaro García Luna accusations were followed by an even more riveting exposé, with Mexico City's ex-chief of federal police accused of being on the take. Guillermo González Calderoni was a legendary figure in Mexico, the model of an upright, incorruptible cop. If Calderoni was leading a double life, as witnesses claimed, he took his secret to his grave: in 2003 Guillermo González Calderoni was shot in the head by an unknown assassin.

The truly stunning revelation thrown up by the trial was the one that never came. When prosecutors announced that Sinaloa Cartel operations chief Jesus Zambada García was ready to name not one but two Mexican presidents in receipt of huge bribes from Guzmán, trial judge Brian M. Cogan shut them down. The reason he gave was that García's accusations would needlessly embarrass a number of 'individuals and entities' not directly connected to the case. Conspiracy theory cover-up specialists had a field day with that one.

One top-ranking politician who was directly accused of corruption was former president Enrique Peña Nieto, Mexico's head of state in 2012–18. He was said to have asked for US$250 million in 2012 in return for calling off a manhunt on Guzmán, who was then on the run. After a few rounds of negotiations his accuser, Colombian drug lord and Guzmán affiliate Alex Cifuentes Villa, said that Nieto settled for US$100 million. This is a charge that Enrique Peña Nieto denies.

As Guzmán's lawyer reasonably pointed out, many of the testimonies at the trial were given in return for lighter sentences and were therefore unreliable. Nevertheless, the evidence against Guzmán was overwhelming and he was found guilty of all charges. As a result, there have been calls to investigate the many allegations levelled against state officials during the trial. Noises have been made in this direction but, at the time of writing, have not been followed through with the alacrity or thoroughness anti-corruption campaigners would desire.

Although Guzmán is behind bars for life, the cycle of violence, corruption and collusion in Mexico continues. With the country's cartels making up to US$29 billion a year, the rewards are simply too tempting to resist and the power of the cartels remains undiminished.

This was illustrated when Guzmán's son, Ovidio, himself a suspected trafficker, was arrested by national guard policemen in the Mexican city of Culiacán in October 2019. What should have been a high-profile success for the government turned into a farce when the 35 police officers holding Guzmán found themselves surrounded by hundreds of Sinaloa Cartel gunmen, or *sicarios*. After a vicious shootout the police were forced to let Guzmán go.

Even if they had taken Ovidio Guzmán in, it would have been a drop in the ocean. Individual narco-criminals come and go, but the narco-state abides.

AMERICAN DEEP STATES TO 1939

SUCH IS THE proliferation of vested interests working to further their own agendas, it might be more accurate to rename the United States of America the United Deep States of America. In this first of two chapters on the USA, we shall look at how the country got there, from the mid-1800s to the eve of World War II. It's a period that witnessed the country begin to realize its enormous economic potential – but as America's commercial growth far exceeded its political development at this time, the situation was ripe for exploitation by the country's avaricious band of 'robber barons' and plutocrats, men whose power derived from their extreme wealth. Beginning with the building of America's railroads, then moving on to the growth of the coal, steel and oil industries, as well as the massive expansion of manufacturing and finance, for those of a deep-state disposition the nation's resources represented a giant Thanksgiving turkey to be carved up among a lucky few.

As America moved into its late-19th century 'Gilded Age' the accumulation of wealth became fetishized, with few questions asked as to where a person's riches had come from and only their success in acquiring it celebrated. When, after 1900, the politicians attempted to assert some authority, the deep states fought back, disregarding or sabotaging government legislation, stepping up their corruption of public officials and, as a last resort with the election of the 'leftist' Franklin D. Roosevelt in 1932, contemplating regime change.

All the while, looking and learning, an ambitious group of criminals was registering the successes of America's corporate deep state and they decided to form one of their own, creating in the mafia the most successful and pervasive organized crime network of modern times.

'ALL ABOARD!' THE GREAT AMERICAN RAILROAD CON

When America's first transcontinental railroad was completed in 1869, it was hailed as a celebration of drive, vigour, engineering excellence and entrepreneurial vision. The railroad was constructed from west to east and from east to west, with the two halves meeting in the middle of America at Promontory Summit in Utah. The western half of the project was the work of the Central Pacific Railroad (CPR) company, while Union Pacific (UP) built the eastern section. Both companies employed dubious and downright criminal business practices to get their work done, with CPR perhaps edging it by a nose – so that's where the focus is here as a deep-state case study.

Leland Stanford and Collis P. Huntingdon were CPR's corruptors-in-chief. Stanford, who was Governor of California in 1861–63, looked after the western end of the operation, in particular by overseeing the passing of state laws to prohibit rival railroad companies from setting up in his territory, ensuring a monopoly for CPR. Huntingdon, meanwhile, was despatched to Washington D.C. with US$200,000 in cash to secure political backing from biddable Congressmen. It was money well spent, as Huntingdon used it to persuade legislators to grant CPR US$24 million in subsidies to get construction underway. Although it was a loan, CPR neglected to return a single penny of it. Armed with free federal cash, and with more on offer, Stanford, Huntingdon and their business partners used the funds to hire building and engineering firms that they secretly owned, so that they were in effect paying themselves.

The sums involved were considerable: US$16,000 for each mile of track built, rising to US$48,000 per mile in the mountains. To make the most of the government's generosity the companies altered the railroad routes, deliberately making them longer and directing them into hilly terrain so that they could charge the higher per-mile fees. Both CPR and UP managed this activity through, respectively,

The Central Pacific Railroad under typically rudimentary construction near Promontory Point, Utah.

the supposedly independent Credit and Finance Corp and Credit Mobilier agencies, which handled the billings and laundered the payments that were collected. When the central government found out about the scam and launched an investigation in 1872, it found that several senators were implicated in railroad corruption. Unfortunately, when government investigators pressed CPR and UP to hand over their accounts both companies reported that their books had been mislaid. When the inquiry then turned its attention to Leland Stanford's conflict of interest and possible abuse of office as the governor of California, they were stymied in court by Justice Stephen Field, a close friend of Stanford's, who ruled that any federal probe into the CPR director was both a violation of the constitution and his civil rights.

It is a shame the companies' accounts went missing, as they could also have shown exactly what CPR and UP did with the 3,640,000 hectares (9,000,000 acres) of land they had been given by the federal government on which to build their tracks. It was understood that the companies would be allowed to sell some of this land in order to offset the cost of constructing the railroad. This was something they certainly did, but they also used the land to repay their backers and supporters for favours and services rendered. The Civil War hero General William T. Sherman was rewarded by UP with large parcels of land in Omaha, Nebraska, for example, after helping to clear the railroad route of Native American tribes who objected to it running through their homelands. UP could not bring itself to give him the land for nothing, though. Instead, they sold it to him for US$2.50 an acre when the market price was US$8.00. This was still a good deal for the military man, who was happy to oblige – after all, his brother Charles T. Sherman was one of Union Pacific's directors. For its part, UP was pleased to number among its friends a national figure as famous as General Sherman, a man touted as a possible future president. This was all the more important as another Sherman brother, John, a senator and in the late 1870s America's treasury secretary, was known to be ambivalent towards large businesses and corporations. In 1890 he successfully introduced the Sherman Anti-Trust Act (see p.182), the intention of which was to deprive companies such as CPR and UP of their monopolistic and cartel-forming power.

Read all about it

With pliable politicians on board and friendly judges on tap, the railroad companies then ensured they were always guaranteed a good press – literally. CPR, for example, purchased the *Sacramento Daily Record* newspaper, and paid the editor and journalists of the rival *Sacramento Union* to print pro-CPR stories. Both periodicals were based in the state capital of California, and their readership included the West Coast's key power-brokers, political elites and regional decision-makers.

But even the CPR's media influence could not bury the story when, in 1883, incriminating correspondence came to light between Collis P. Huntingdon and David Colton, one of CPR's financial directors. The letters laid bare CPR's full programme of bribery and political collusion, leaving Americans in little doubt as to the type of men Huntingdon, Stanford and their fellow CPR owners were. However, as the letters did not contain the names of anyone who had been in receipt of bribes, Huntingdon escaped prosecution. It was a chastening experience, though, and it broke the first rule of deep-state etiquette: never put yourself in the centre of the story. Following publication of the letters, CPR's directors scaled down their underhand activities. Two years later, Leland Stanford bought himself a seat in the United States Senate, and two years after that established Stanford University. He died in 1893 and was mourned as a pioneering captain of industry and a generous philanthropist. The same applied to Huntingdon, who died in 1900.

Yet by the time they died, the railroads that Stanford and Huntingdon built were already in trouble. The cost-shaving and theft perpetrated by the Central Pacific Railroad, Union Pacific and other rail companies meant that less than 20 years after the transcontinental railroad was completed, much of the nation's tracks had to be ripped up and relaid. This was in part because the railroad companies never agreed at the outset which track gauge to employ, so they all laid rails of different shapes and sizes. Where railroads with different track gauges met, passengers and freight had to be taken off one train and moved to another. In Ohio, the railroad companies were not prepared to pay the high cost of bridging the Ohio River, so they simply built track on either side of it, forcing locomotive users to detrain and use ferries.

Bridges built in the early days of the railroad were often of inferior quality. The 200 m (650 ft) Dale Creek Crossing bridge in Wyoming was completed in 1868. It should have been constructed in iron but, to save money, was built of wood instead. This meant that it swayed alarmingly in high winds and could hardly bear the

The construction of the bridge at Dale Creek Crossing in 1868. It was built out of wood rather than iron to save money – and was subsequently rebuilt twice.

weight of heavy freight trains. It had to be rebuilt – partially, again to save money – in 1876, and once more in 1885. In general, safety measures were non-existent, being seen as an unnecessary expense to protect labourers who were largely imported from China and considered expendable. Tunnel collapses, fatal mudslides and embankment subsidence were common, as were train derailments because sleepers were rarely laid on stabilizing track ballast and the rails themselves were made from lower-grade, lighter and cheaper metal which broke and buckled easily.

When the results of this shoddy and corner-cutting approach started coming to light from the 1870s onwards, the federal government refused to offer any financial help. It was, after all, still waiting in vain for the repayment of its original US$24 million subsidy. Instead, the railwaymen turned to private capital to bail them out and walked straight into the arms of the financier J.P. Morgan. By the end of the century the New York-based J.P. Morgan and Huhn, Loeb and Co. investment banks had bought up most of America's major railroad networks, grouping them together into five major companies.

THE RISE OF BIG BUSINESS

The role of John Pierpont Morgan in 'saving' America's railroads points to his position as the robber baron/inspirational entrepreneur par excellence of the country's so-called Gilded Age. Born into an affluent banking family in 1837, Morgan entered the finance business aged 20. By the beginning of the 1890s he was one of the richest men in America, and his intervention in the railroad industry is indicative of how he got there. Morgan was, in short, the great consolidator. Whenever he involved himself in an industrial sector, be it banking, railways or steel production, Morgan's aim was always to take over a number of small companies and fuse them together to create monopolies rather than foster competition.

For Morgan and his fellow plutocrats such as the Scottish-American steel magnate Andrew Carnegie and the oilman John

D. Rockefeller, their fortunes were so vast that money was almost irrelevant to them. Whereas figures such as Leland Stanford and Collis P. Huntingdon had been driven to establish deep state networks in order to further their accumulation of wealth, J.P. Morgan *et al* were more interested in protecting what they had and, just as importantly, in exercising real power – not openly, and therefore accountably, but in secret, behind the scenes and by means of deep state influence.

Around the time that Morgan was buying up America's railroads, there was a growing concern that some big businesses were becoming too big, and that monopolies and cartels were beginning to form, stifling competition and innovation by setting up restrictive associations known as trusts. This resulted in 1890 with the passing of the Sherman Anti-Trust Act, a measure introduced precisely to take on America's monopolies and cartels – except that it didn't. In fact, what should have been an era-defining piece of legislation that saw America's politicians take back regulatory control of the country's economy became instead a shining example of the deep states' ability to disregard the country's laws and act as they saw fit.

A blatant example of this came in 1895, when the Sherman Act was used against the American Sugar Company (ASC), which processed 95 per cent of sugar sold in the USA. ASC was clearly operating as a monopoly, but it argued that, as a manufacturer, it was not subject to the Sherman Act, which only covered trade and commerce. Caught out by this technicality, the Supreme Court had no choice but to rule in ASC's favour. Inspired by ASC's examples, America's other monopolistic corporations pored over the Sherman Act in search of get-out clauses they too could exploit. It turned out they were in luck. The Sherman Act was poorly worded and had been hastily drawn up in response to public pressure to do something about the country's business cartels. The corporations' expensively retained lawyers were in most cases easily able to circumvent the Sherman Act on the rare occasions it was

J.P. Morgan, America's most successful banker and financier during the country's Gilded Age.

deployed, which was just 18 times in its first 10 years, and never successfully against any large businesses.

However, it was not a lack of expectation for a successful outcome that discouraged successive attorney-generals from taking on the cartels; it was more that their deep state ties to the big corporations ensured it was not in their interests to do so. Richard Olney, attorney-general at the time of the ASC case, was widely seen as a robber-baron man. Before joining the government of

John Sherman, author of the 1890 Sherman Anti-Trust Act, which is still in use today.

President Grover Cleveland in 1893, he had been a director and legal counsel for several railroad companies. When he became attorney-general, Olney secured an assurance that he would still be able to represent his railroad interests, from which he drew an annual salary of US$10,000 to add to his government wage of US$8,000. While this was a clear conflict of interest, things took a more profound deep-state turn when Olney used the Sherman Act against striking union workers at the Pullman railway coach factory in 1894, arguing that industrial action constituted restraint of trade, which was proscribed by the Sherman Act. The strike leaders were arrested, the Pullman workers were ordered back to work, and Olney's railroad employers were delighted that their inside man had represented their interests so assiduously. The precedent set, the Sherman Act was used a further three times against striking workers in the 1890s.

A few years later, in 1897, Joseph McKenna was appointed attorney-general under the Republican president William McKinley. Like Olney before him, McKenna was a long-time deep-state asset. Originally based in California, he had been a loyal supporter of Leland Stanford during his governorship of the state. In return, Stanford sponsored McKenna's political ambitions and helped him to a seat in Congress in 1885, where he steadfastly represented the robber barons' deep-state interests by opposing business regulations and voting for extending government subsidies to the railroads. McKenna carried his pro-commerce agenda into his time as attorney-general, blocking any attempts to prosecute the corporations under the Sherman Act. So ineffective was the Act that in 1890–1900 the number of trusts increased from 251 to 290, and the money invested in them rose from US$192 million to US$326 million.

VOTING WITH THEIR WALLETS

The campaign that secured the presidency for McKenna's Republican Party leader William McKinley in 1896 is now recognized as the first modern election, utilizing the power of the press, marketing, attack ads, voter-targeting and other practices that are now commonplace. The plutocrats were involved, of course, contributing a then-record amount of US$4 million in campaign funds that dwarfed the US$300,000 war chest of McKinley's Democratic opponent, William Jennings Bryan. The conduit between the robber barons' millions and Republican coffers was the millionaire businessman and senator Mark Hanna, who, as well as being a former high-school classmate of John D. Rockefeller, was also McKinley's campaign manager (and puppet-master, according to the press). The robber barons' millions propelled McKinley to the Oval Office in 1896, and again in 1900. In return, they got a staunchly pro-business president who maintained high tariffs against cheap imported foreign goods and was suitably disinclined to listen to popular calls to address the power of the plutocrats.

In September 1901, William McKinley was assassinated by Leon Czolgosz, an anarchist gunman who believed that all forms of government were illegitimate. While Czolgosz's was an extreme act, it reflected a growing unease in American society that the needs of ordinary men and women were being disregarded in favour of big business. McKinley's replacement in office, vice-president Theodore Roosevelt, picked up on this straight away. Roosevelt was a populist by nature and announced he would be a trust-busting president. This won him enormous public support and Roosevelt made great play of his fight against the plutocrats. But 'play' is the operative word here. Roosevelt was a skilful politician and he reassured business elites that for every public assault upon them perpetrated through the Sherman Act there would be a private, secretly delivered recompense. For example, when he used the anti-trust law in 1902 to break up the Northern Securities Company railroad cartel established by J.P. Morgan and the railwaymen James J. Hill and E.H. Harriman, Roosevelt ensured the injured parties were generously compensated for the losses they had incurred. This allowed the president to cash in the political dividend of appearing tough on the cartels while ensuring those same cartels kept their Republican Party donations coming. When this arrangement was uncovered by the press after Roosevelt had been returned as president in the 1904 election, he brazened it out and dismissed the journalists who had exposed him as 'muckrakers'.

Nevertheless, Roosevelt's popularity was damaged by the revelations, and in an effort to regain his 'man of the people' reputation, he approved the Tillman Act of 1907, a law that banned corporations from making direct donations to federal election campaigns. As with the Sherman Anti-Trust Act, the Tillman Act was far from perfect. The plutocrats quickly found ways around it and, having passed a bill that threatened to cut off its money supply, Congress showed little enthusiasm for enforcing it. Slowly, over time, the rules were tightened further still, but this only drove campaign funding underground, making deep-state activity more rather than less likely.

Roosevelt decided not to stand for re-election in 1908 and the presidency was won by his fellow Republican, William Howard Taft. While Taft was, like Roosevelt, a popularity-seeking trust-buster, unlike Roosevelt he was a poor tactician, especially in his inability to keep the plutocrats on side. In his single four-year term in office, Taft employed the Sherman Act more than 70 times – double the figure Roosevelt racked up in seven years. For the robber barons, Taft became public enemy number one. Not that he cared – he believed he did not need the plutocrats' money and that his populist appeal would overcome any obstacles they put in his way. It was a disastrous miscalculation. Theodore Roosevelt was as horrified by Taft's trust-busting zeal as the robber barons and ran as a rival Progressive Party candidate against him in the 1912 presidential election. This split the vote and secured victory for the Democrat Woodrow Wilson, who remained in office for the next eight years.

THE MAN WHO HAD IT ALL

As a parting shot to the robber barons, Taft's administration delivered what was supposed to be a damning verdict against the biggest corporation of all, Standard Oil. Ultimately, however, the use of the Sherman Anti-Trust Act against the company in 1911 turned its owner, John D. Rockefeller, from an extremely rich man into the richest man on Earth.

John D. Rockefeller was the embodiment of the American dream. Born to a travelling salesman and con-artist father in 1839, he inherited the paternal gene for doing deals, shady or otherwise. He started his first business aged 20 and established what would become Standard Oil in 1870. Over the next 27 years, Rockefeller built up the company until it controlled up to 90 per cent of America's oil business. How Rockefeller achieved that dominance was what landed Standard Oil in the anti-trust dock in 1911. Rockefeller had retired from running the company by then, but he remained its largest shareholder and Standard Oil was run very much in his image.

We know all about Standard Oil's monopolistic ways thanks to the journalistic endeavours of Ida Tarbell, one of Theodore Roosevelt's 'muckrakers', who, in a painstakingly compiled series of 19 articles for the magazine *McClure's* beginning in 1902, laid out Standard Oil's recipe for success. First, the company would spy on its rivals to gain valuable inside information. Then it would deliberately discount its product prices to force smaller rivals out of business or to compel them to sell out to Rockefeller, an illegal practice outlawed by the Interstate Commerce Act of 1887. Tarbell reminded her readers that, in 1892, courts in Standard Oil's then-home state of Ohio had declared the company a trust and ordered it be dissolved. Rockefeller responded by ignoring the court and moving his company to New York City. In the process, Standard Oil reorganized itself into a complex network of shell companies, fronts and legal structures that obscured the company's ownership and accounts. Tarbell, dubbed 'Miss Tarbarrel' by Rockefeller and 'this poison woman' by Theodore Roosevelt, also revealed how Standard Oil bribed and blackmailed government officials so that it could continue to operate with impunity.

Confronted with these revelations, and mindful of his self-designated reputation as a trust-buster, in 1905 Roosevelt ordered his justice department to investigate Standard Oil under the Sherman Act – but not too vigorously. This, and the stalling tactics of Standard Oil's attorneys, meant that it was a full six years before the inquiry was completed, during the administration of the enthusiastically anti-trust-minded President Taft. The investigation report was damning, containing evidence of price fixing, industrial espionage, bribery, corruption and blackmail that left the Supreme Court with no option but to declare Standard Oil an illegal trust. The organization was given six months to disincorporate itself into 34 separate and unconnected companies in order to end its illegal monopoly.

But the law of unintended consequences had a joke to play on the law of the land. No sooner had Standard Oil been taken apart than it was found that the 34 new companies were collectively more profitable than the single giant corporation they had once comprised. As John D. Rockefeller remained the largest shareholder in all of the new businesses, he found that his wealth had increased greatly. In one fell swoop Rockefeller became America's first billionaire. Over the next few years his ever-increasing wealth made him the richest person on the planet and one of the most affluent men in history. In modern terms his personal fortune was around US$350–400 billion, more than three times that of Amazon founder Jeff Bezos, the richest man on Earth today. Furthermore, the breaking up of Standard Oil resulted in some of its 34 'children' growing into companies that would become BP, Chevron and ExxonMobil.

As for John D. Rockefeller, happily retired and newly mega-rich, he devoted the rest of his long life to philanthropy and died, aged 97, on 23 May 1937.

FROM WARREN G. HARDING TO FDR

The breaking up of Standard Oil, followed swiftly by World War I, marked the end of an era for the plutocrats and their grand, sweeping plans for deep-state dominance. By 1918 many of the old robber barons were dead, retired, or had reinvented themselves as born-again philanthropists and had been replaced by a new generation of entrepreneurs with less ambitious intentions or calculating minds. The Republican Warren G. Harding won the 1920 presidential election on the campaign slogan 'A Return To Normalcy', and that's what most Americans wanted. A post-war economic boom ensured that a string of forgettable Republican presidents occupied the Oval Office, marking time and letting the country run itself. In this way, there was no real need for corporate deep states to proliferate, as they had a free hand anyway.

There was corruption, of course, but it was of the common or garden variety. Much of it was focused around the so-called 'Ohio Gang', who were the friends, political associates and businessmen gathered around Warren G. Harding, whose short presidency – he died in office in 1923 – was filled with incidents and allegations of dishonesty. The Ohio Gang met for regular poker nights at a Washington D.C. building known as the Little Green House on K Street. Members of Harding's cabinet, such as the interior secretary Albert Fall and the attorney-general Harry Daugherty, would spend long evenings in the proverbial smoke-filled rooms playing high-stakes games of chance with predatory businessmen.

Among these were the oilmen Harry Sinclair and Edward Doheny, who in 1922 bribed Fall to give them exclusive and illegally acquired access to government-owned oil reserves at a place in Wyoming called Teapot Dome (which gave the resulting scandal its name) and California's Elk Hills and Buena Vista Hills. Fall was convicted of accepting bribes after the scandal broke in 1924 and was sentenced to a year in prison. He holds the honour of being the first American to be convicted of a felony while holding a cabinet post. In retrospect, it's surprising it took that long. Sinclair and

Warren Harding (first left) at his first cabinet meeting, including Ohio Gang members Harry Daugherty (third left) and Albert Fall (fourth right).

Doheny, meanwhile, were found not guilty, although Sinclair was sentenced to six months on a related contempt of court charge. Harry Daugherty was also implicated in the Teapot Dome scandal, and in several other corruption cases, but always managed to avoid conviction.

By the end of the 1920s, however, there was a lot less cash to share in profits or kickbacks to politicians and public officials. The Wall Street Crash of 1929 saw to that, ushering in a decade-long global depression that was only resolved by the outbreak of World War II. But while the Depression caused America's deep states to lie low, the victory of the Democrat Franklin D. Roosevelt in the 1932 presidential election stirred them into one, admittedly half-hearted, reaction. Before FDR, six of the previous seven presidents had all been Republicans who were all in their different ways amenable to deep-state influence. FDR was not, or at least certain sections of the corporate deep state were not prepared to wait around to find out if he was.

In late 1934, the government-appointed McCormack-Dickstein Committee was convened to investigate allegations of a plot to overthrow the president. A retired Marine called Major-General Smedley Butler claimed he had been recruited by a group of financiers, bankers and industrialists to front a coup to overthrow

FDR and establish an authoritarian regime along the lines of those recently come to power in Hitler's Germany and Mussolini's Italy. Among the names mentioned in testimony before the committee were the Wall Street banker Grayson M.P. Murphy and Robert Sterling Clark, the Singer Sewing Machine heir. Butler also implicated the American Liberty League, a body set up in 1934 in opposition to FDR's left-leaning New Deal policies. Its leading lights included Alfred P. Sloan, the CEO of General Motors, J. Howard Pew of the Sun Oil Company, Al Smith, the former governor of New York, ex-secretary of state Elihu Root, and the banker and soon-to-be Connecticut senator Prescott Bush, father and grandfather of future Republican presidents George H. W. Bush and George W. Bush.

All those named as part of what was dubbed the 'Business Plot' denied any involvement, claiming that General Butler was a fantasist. Not one of them was called to testify before the committee, and the only 'plot' participant it did question was a Wall Street bond trader called Gerald MacGuire, who Butler alleged was his go-between with the coup plotters. MacGuire denied everything, repeating the party line that Butler was a fantasist. He was unable to elaborate any further as he died of pneumonia the following year, aged 38.

The Business Plot was written off at the time as backroom talk by a few zealous patriots over-reacting to the election of the 'leftist' FDR; all of the star names attached to it had simply been added by General Butler to give his paranoid fantasies credibility, it was claimed. In the years following his allegations against the Business Plot conspirators, Butler did little to refute this version of events, going on to publish a book called *War Is A Racket* and becoming an outspoken critic of what would later be called the military-industrial complex, indicating perhaps a cast of mind not entirely in harmony with the men he claimed had tried to recruit him to overthrow the president. But historians and journalists have since confirmed that the Business Plot was real and that at the least

Major-General Smedley Butler, who claimed he was recruited by US business leaders to oversee a coup against President Franklin Roosevelt.

its conspirators wanted to impose a business-friendly co-president alongside FDR to ensure their interests were represented at the highest levels of government – and that in Smedley Butler they had simply chosen the wrong man to execute their plan.

THE ITALIAN CONNECTION

While the corporate corruptions of the 1920s and the financial conspiracies of the early 1930s were taking place, another deep state was emerging in a different sector of society and it was one that would have a lasting and overwhelmingly negative effect on American life: the mafia.

Things would almost certainly have turned out differently had it not been for Prohibition. The fact that America's politicians approved a ban on the manufacture, transportation and sale of alcohol from 1920 until 1933 is hard to credit today but, lobbied hard by religious and morally motivated groups such as the Women's Christian Temperance Movement and the Anti-Saloon League, that's exactly what Congress did, having been convinced by anti-alcohol campaigners that the demon drink was the root cause of most of the crimes committed in America.

But as soon as the Volstead Act banning alcohol took effect in January 1920, the country experienced a crime wave the likes of which it had never seen before or since. Just because alcohol was no longer available it did not mean that Americans no longer wanted to drink it. Quite the opposite. In no time at all bootleggers were smuggling spirits and beer across the border from Canada and Mexico, and moonshiners were brewing up infernally potent concoctions of hooch and rotgut, unregulated by law and regardless of concerns for the health and safety of the consumer. Illegal speakeasies and drinking dens sprang up in basements and back rooms across the land, catering to thirsty Americans willing to pay over the odds for their alcohol of choice. This entire underground infrastructure developed organically at first, with local 'entrepreneurs' responding to local needs, but in just a few years it came to be dominated by a network of loosely affiliated criminal gangs of mostly Italian descent that, in time, grew ever closer to become the mafia.

Between 1880 and 1920, around four million Italians, most of them from the poverty-stricken south and Sicily, emigrated to the US and settled in New York and Chicago in particular. These communities were insular at first and were preyed upon by small gangs of their fellow countrymen who ran gambling and lottery, or 'numbers', syndicates (always a lucrative business among poorer populations), or who offered 'protection' to Italian tradesmen and businesses. It's arguable that these gangs would have remained small-scale had it not been for the enormous criminal opportunities offered by Prohibition. Neighbourhood mobs such as New York's Black Hand and the Five Points Gang, which operated in the Big Apple as well as Chicago, jumped on the Prohibition bandwagon and got very rich in double-quick time. Barely literate strong-arm men such as Al Capone in Chicago and Giuseppe 'Joe the Boss' Masseria in New York found themselves elevated into regional crime lords and they revelled in their notoriety, flaunting their wealth and power in public across the 1920s while embarking on a bitter power struggle for control of the illegal alcohol business that played out across America's major cities.

Eventually, the criminal gangs realized that fighting each other was counter-productive. By the time Al Capone was jailed on tax evasion charges in 1931, the criminal bosses were already moving towards a more sophisticated and lower-profile approach to business. Men such as Charles 'Lucky' Luciano and the Polish-Jewish Meyer Lansky came to the fore. These were men not just interested in making money; these were men with a plan, who saw that targeting power structures was the way forward. Luciano and Lansky joined with other Italian-American and also Jewish and Irish mobs to come together in 1929 as the National Crime Syndicate or, simply, 'the Syndicate' – the first truly organized crime network in America. Control of the major cities and regions was divided among several crime 'families' and Luciano established the Commission as the mafia's governing body to settle disputes. Learning quickly from their corporate deep-state counterparts, this growing mafia bribed, corrupted and intimidated judges, police and politicians into allowing them to go about their business. Those who resisted were murdered. The profits involved were enormous and, during the Depression from 1929 onwards, it was difficult for cash-strapped public officials to say no to free money – especially when the alternative option was a bullet to the head.

By the time Prohibition was repealed in 1933, the mafia genie was well and truly out of the bottle. With alcohol legal again, this sophisticated crime network was hardly likely to be satisfied with its old practices of neighbourhood numbers-running and protection rackets (though they continued to do those also). Drugs, entertainment and large-scale gambling were the coming things, and the mafia deep state was determined to get in on the ground floor. It did just that, permeating all aspects of American culture, commerce and politics. In fact, following World War II, all of the varieties of deep state encountered in this chapter, plus several more, evolved, adapted and expanded in ways that have made them dangerously powerful and virtually unassailable.

CHAPTER 8

POST-WAR AMERICAN DEEP STATES

SINCE THE END of World War II, traditional vested interests such as corporate deep states and the intelligence services have diversified and evolved into more sophisticated entities such as the military-industrial complex and the 'national security state'. Self-interested agendas, hidden or otherwise, are being pushed, so that the first question any seasoned observer of American politics should ask on the introduction of any new government legislation is: who benefits?

This chapter navigates a path through the crowded field of arms manufacturers, intelligence networks, major corporations, media groups, lobbyists, think tanks and the administrative arm of the state itself as they compete and collude to further their own aims. This is by necessity only a partial picture: organized crime and organized religion, for example, are not discussed, although their deep-state influence is undeniably strong. The focus here is on the vested interests with the most influence over public life in America in modern times. We'll see also how the election of Donald Trump as president in 2016 temporarily rearranged the behind-the-scenes balance of power – and how the ever-resourceful deep states fought back.

THE MILITARY-INDUSTRIAL COMPLEX

America emerged from World War II having manufactured its way out of the Depression and into prosperity. For the next 30 years, the country experienced unprecedented growth and developed into the wealthiest and most powerful nation on Earth. The key, everyone agreed in those golden years, was for the federal government to take a back seat and allow business to do what it did best, which was to make money.

One area where there was much money to be made was defence. As one war ended in 1945 another one began – a Cold War that lasted for almost 50 years and which also saw 'hot' conflicts in Korea and Vietnam, as well as oil wars in the Middle East from the 1990s and the ongoing War on Terror of today. But the arms market is highly competitive and, with billions of dollars on offer, its key players are well versed in deep-state strategies in order to gain a competitive advantage.

Arms and the men

In his farewell address to the nation on 17 January 1961, outgoing Republican president Dwight D. Eisenhower warned his fellow Americans to be wary of a new power in the land. 'In the councils of government, we must guard against the acquisition of unwarranted influence, whether sought or unsought, by the military-industrial complex,' he said. 'The potential for the disastrous rise of misplaced power exists and will persist.'

But Eisenhower's admonition came too late. By the beginning of the 1960s the military-industrial complex of arms manufacturers and military elites with big budgets to maintain was already firmly dug in. In the 15 years since D-Day America had barely been at peace, its armed forces having deployed in the Korean War and in various crises in Jerusalem, Berlin, China, Taiwan, Puerto Rico, Egypt, Lebanon and Vietnam. All the while, ongoing tensions with the Soviet Union meant that full-scale nuclear conflict was a permanent possibility. The USA needed its arms, but probably not as many as it was sold. Throughout the 1950s, for example, both the CIA and America's military establishment deliberately overestimated the Soviet Union's fighting capacities: in 1959, America's intelligence services told the White House Russia possessed an estimated 1,000–1,500 nuclear missiles, compared to the USA's 100. In reality, the Soviet Union had just four atomic bombs. Unaware of this, the Department of Defense went on a spending spree worth billions of dollars to close the non-existent 'missile gap' with Russia. Among the beneficiaries were the missile manufacturers Convair Group and the Glenn L. Martin Company, which later became part of the giant corporations General Dynamics and Lockheed Martin respectively.

Throughout the Cold War and up to the present, General Dynamics and Lockheed Martin, along with the contractors Northrop Grumman, Boeing and Raytheon, have dominated military construction and are known as the 'big five'. All, on numerous occasions, have been charged with acts of bribery, corruption and criminal activity, and all have taken part in deep-state actions in order to guarantee their slice of a US defence budget that, as of 2019, stood at US$716 billion.

Lockheed Martin is the world's largest defence contractor, with sales of US$59 billion in 2019. One of its favourite ploys when winning US military contracts is to massively overcharge or fraudulently bill for the work it does, something for which it has been fined or censured on several occasions, including 1998 (US$3.15 million), 2002 (US$2.1 million), 2003 (three instances, with fines totalling US$46.6 million), 2005 (US$1.4 million), 2007 (a US$265 million fine for 'inadvertent' overbilling) and 2012 (US$15.85 million). This is only a partial list, and it's a practice all the big five have been charged with. These false billing and overcharge offences are possible because of the companies' ability to induce military and defence officials to cover up their activities and provide privileged or secret information. This means that the big five have been able to go beyond 'simple' accountancy irregularities to something darker and deeper.

In 2011, Lockheed Martin made a US$2 million settlement against allegations it had illegally obtained inside information in relation to a contract competition with the US Navy. In this, Lockheed Martin was following in the footsteps of Boeing, whose military aircraft division was fined US$5 million in 1989 for illicitly obtaining classified Pentagon planning papers. Earlier still, Northrop Grumman in the mid-1980s was accused, among other things, of paying the dog-kennel fees and country club

The house that war built: the Virginia offices of aerospace and defence giant Lockheed Martin, just outside Washington D.C.

memberships of Pentagon officials in return for information and favourable consideration on contract bids. Raytheon was also trading on insider knowledge in the 1980s, and in 1990 pleaded guilty and was fined US$1 million for trafficking in stolen Pentagon budget plans.

You scratch my back . . .

Yet for all their crimes and misdemeanours, the major military contractors keep winning government contracts. This is undoubtedly because they have the requisite manufacturing capabilities, but also because they have the right personnel.

A little like the system that obtains in the upper echelons of France's political, commercial and civil service elites (see pp.43–9), America's defence industry is populated with 'revolver' executives who move between the worlds of commerce, politics and civil administration and where networks of friendship, favour-trading, contacts, know-how, inside information and occasionally corruption ensure the priorities of the military-industrial complex are always well represented. Since 2000, Boeing's defence arm has spent more than US$275 million on lobbying and in 2016–19, for example, recruited 19 retired high-level military officials as consultants, board members or lobbyists. In the decade up to 2019 the big five hired 25 retired generals, 9 admirals, 43 lieutenant-generals and 23 vice-admirals.

When they are not hiring former military men, the arms' manufacturers recruit from government and the civil service, usually targeting the House and Senate Appropriations Subcommittees that allocate federal defence spending. The traffic goes the other way, too, with high-ranking defence contractor executives accepting government posts, bringing with them the interests and objectives of their former employers. Occasionally, deals are made when employees are in transit between the worlds of government and industry: in 2003 Boeing's chief financial officer was fired when it emerged he had offered a job to an Air Force procurement executive while the two parties were negotiating a US$20 billion supply contract.

For one very high-profile example of how the military-industrial revolving door system works, consider the career of Dick Cheney. A Republican political insider since the early 1970s, in 1989 Cheney was appointed secretary of defence under President George H. W. Bush. Out of a job after Bush lost the 1992 presidential election to the Democrat Bill Clinton, Cheney passed through the revolving door to become CEO of the oil, gas, construction and military services corporation Halliburton. After George W. Bush won the 2000 presidential election Cheney 'revolved' again, signing on as Bush's vice-president, an appointment that coincided with the 9/11 al-Qaeda attacks.

During Cheney's eight-year vice-presidency, Halliburton profited handsomely from America's post-9/11 War on Terror. Before Cheney took office, Halliburton was the 22nd largest military contractor in America; by 2003 it was seventh, having been awarded US government contracts worth up to US$7 billion in Afghanistan, Iraq and elsewhere, mostly expedited by Halliburton's building, engineering and services subsidiary Kellogg Brown & Root (KBR) – known colloquially in US defence circles as 'Kellogg Burn & Loot'. In 2004, *Time* magazine obtained an Army Corps of Engineers email that appeared to confirm that KBR had won most of its contracting work without going through any bidding processes, with the knowledge of Dick Cheney's office. This prompted the 2004 Democratic presidential candidate John Kerry to claim that 'Dick Cheney's old company Halliburton has profited from the mess in Iraq at the expense of American troops and taxpayers. While Halliburton has been engaging in massive overcharging and wasteful practices under this no-bid contract, Dick Cheney has continued to receive compensation from his former company.'

Aside from strategic recruitment, the other main tactic the military-industrial deep state deploys is the use of lobbying. In 1983, companies and interest groups spent about US$200 million on lobbying; by 2018 it was US$3.4 billion. To give just one not atypical example, from 1993 to 2015 Howard 'Buck' McKeon was a Republican Congressman whose California district contained several military bases and defence-related manufacturing facilities. This, and McKeon's position as chair of the powerful Armed Services Committee, meant that his re-election campaigns every four years were generously supported by, among others, Lockheed Martin, Northrop Grumman, General Dynamics and Boeing. After leaving politics in 2015, the former Congressman set up the McKeon Group, a lobbying firm whose clients include Lockheed Martin and General Dynamics. The McKeon group also lobbies on behalf of the Saudi Arabian government, to whom US arms' sales doubled under McKeon's chairmanship of the Armed Services Committee.

Gamekeepers turned poachers

None of McKeon's activities are illegal, but even where there are laws they can usually be circumvented, not just by the military-industrial complex but by all organizations involved in lobbying and campaign contribution-giving. According to the 1995 Lobbying Disclosure Act and the 2007 Honest Leadership and Open Government Act, interest groups must declare how much they spend on lobbying, while all political office holders and civil servants are required to wait for up to two years after leaving public service before becoming lobbyists. But an ex-Congressman or sub-committee chair-holder can leave their government posts on Friday and begin work as lobbyists on Monday if they simply redesignate themselves as consultants, a tactic employed by the former House Speakers Newt Gingrich and John Boehner in the 2000s. Boehner in particular has a history in this area, and in 1995 was criticized for handing out campaign contribution cheques from the tobacco lobby to Republican colleagues in the House of Representatives chamber. In 2010 a *New York Times* story highlighted Boehner's close links to several businesses, including Goldman Sachs, Citigroup, Google, MillerCoors (now Molson Coors) and UPS.

Buck McKeon, the well-connected former Republican Congressman-turned corporate lobbyist.

The representation of corporate interests in politics is not always as clear as the *New York Times* portrait of John Boehner suggests, however, and millions of dollars are regularly filtered through 'dark money' channels which are exempt from lobbying disclosure regulations. These include registered charities, trusts and trade associations – particularly the US Chamber of Commerce, which acts as a kind of clearing house for lobbying funds and campaign donations whose exact origins corporations would prefer to be kept secret.

Until 2010, how politicians were funded when standing for office was strictly regulated, notably by the Tillman Act of 1907 (see p.187), which banned corporations from making direct donations to political campaigns. This changed in 2010, when the Supreme Court upheld a complaint by the conservative pressure group Citizens United that this was unconstitutional. Following the Citizens United decision, corporations, groups and individuals were free to provide unlimited campaign funding through the creation of political action committees (PACs), where interested parties pool their resources to maximize their leverage over their favoured candidates. For added cover, PACs are still free to use dark money channels to make their donations.

CORPORATE DEEP STATES

To see how corporate deep states in particular 'game' the political system in both the pre- and post-Citizens United eras, it's worth looking at the most politically powerful family most people have probably never heard of. It's easy to look at corporate deep-state pressure in America in terms of the large and globally famous multinationals such as Exxon Mobil in oil, Ford in automobile production, or Pfizer in pharmaceuticals. Exxon Mobil, for example, was no doubt delighted when Rex Tillerson, their CEO in 2006–17, was appointed secretary of state in 2018. Yet beyond, or beneath, such visible translations of business interest into political influence lies something far more significant, where even profits play second fiddle to a far more important motive: ideology.

No rules, no regulations

For 50 years, Charles Koch has been the driving force behind Koch Industries, a vast conglomerate embracing oil refining and the production of chemicals, plastics, nitrogen fertilizer, paper and many other unglamorous but vital products and services. As of 2019, the Wichita-based company's revenues were US$119 billion. But Koch Industries is more than a corporation; it is an expression of Charles Koch's self-created philosophy of Market-Based Management (MBM), an uncompromising fusion of political libertarianism and economic freedom. Since the early 1970s, Charles Koch has been exerting his deep-state influence to reshape American politics and society so that they reflect his vision of a country where there is no taxation, widespread business deregulation (especially concerning emissions), no welfare or health provision and the reduction of government to a purely 'night watchman' capacity.

An almost perfect case study of Koch's MBM machine at work was shown in its role in the fight against Donald Trump's controversial tax reforms of 2017. Although the president trumpeted his Tax Cuts and Jobs Act as a business-friendly bill, Charles Koch opposed it on the grounds it was not friendly to his own business. A provision in the bill known as the Border Adjustment Tax (BAT) raised levies against companies that imported many of their raw materials – companies such as Koch Industries.

Koch Industries' mission was to get BAT removed from the bill, and it used all of the deep-state dark arts to do it. First, it unleashed its 'shock troops', a pressure group the company covertly funded and controlled called Americans for Prosperity (AfP), to knock on doors, go leafleting, make phone calls and disrupt public hearings and political meetings to loudly protest against what it called Trump's 'crony capitalism' and 'economy rigging', a charge that stung the famously thin-skinned president. Then, sympathetic experts were hired to appear on television or pen op-ed pieces describing how the tax would mean higher prices for imported goods such as toys, electronics and, most alarmingly, gasoline. Finally, senators and House of Representative members in receipt of Koch Industries funding were reminded that donations could just as easily be withdrawn as granted. Among these were Paul Ryan, Speaker of the House of Representatives and one of the tax bill's sponsors.

Confronted with both public and political pressure, Trump backed down. BAT was removed from the bill and Koch Industries called off the attacks. Just days after the Koch-friendly legislation was signed into law in December 2017, Paul Ryan's PAC received a US$500,000 donation from Charles Koch. It has been estimated that the amended act will save Koch Industries US$1 billion annually.

Koch Industries secured its tax concession from Donald Trump by earlier executing a strategic masterstroke in opposing the president's plans to repeal the Affordable Care Act, commonly known as 'Obamacare'. Ordinarily, Charles Koch would happily have destroyed any legislation that imposed state-provided healthcare. But in this case he deliberately deployed the AfP and threatened to defund Congressmen and women to give Donald Trump a preview of the power he had at his disposal, which he could use to ensure the total defeat of the upcoming tax reforms if he did not get his way.

Charles Koch was aided in his efforts to influence the president by the insertion of well-placed sympathizers in the Trump camp. These included Corey Lewandowski, Kellyanne Conway and Don McGahn, Donald Trump's campaign manager, spokesperson and personal lawyer respectively, as well as Alan Cobb, the AfP vice-president, who joined the Trump team as a senior advisor. It should be noted that Kellyanne Conway and other Team Trump figures also had links to Robert Mercer, the publicity-shy hedge-fund

The most powerful man you've never heard of: industrialist and fervent libertarian Charles Koch.

billionaire who shares Charles Koch's deregulatory, free-market zeal; he owns the right-wing Breitbart news network and brought Steve Bannon into Donald Trump's inner circle. Mercer also part-owned Cambridge Analytica, the political consulting firm at the centre of allegations into possible Russian interference in Trump's successful 2016 electoral campaign and the UK Brexit vote of 2017 (see pp.68–9).

All of these techniques and more had been honed by Koch Industries during the presidency of Barack Obama (2009–17), especially when the Democrat administration tried to introduce the so-called Clean Air Act, a piece of emissions-limiting legislation the Koch family believed posed an existential threat to their oil-refining, plastics-making business empire. Republican politicians who did not wholeheartedly oppose the Clean Air Act were subjected to AfP protests, media attacks, the withdrawal of campaign contributions and, ultimately, deselection. This was the fate of Bob Inglis, a 12-year Congressman whose failure to toe Koch Industries' line saw him replaced as the Republican candidate for South Carolina's 4th District in 2010 by the Koch-funded Trey Gowdie. In this period Charles Koch also harnessed the disruptive power of the grassroots anti-taxation, anti-regulatory Tea Party movement, organized by AfP activists and part-funded by Koch Industries and tobacco giants Philip Morris and R.J. Reynolds. In 2010, alongside the Koch-endorsed Trey Gowdie, the mid-term Congressional elections saw 85 new Republicans elected, 57 of whom had been funded by Koch Industries. This ended the Democrats' majority in the House of Representatives and, effectively, killed any chance of the Clean Air Act passing.

Power to the people

In terms of mobilizing grassroots support, one organization that possibly outranks Koch Industries is the National Rifle Association (NRA). Founded in 1871, the NRA is one of America's oldest and most powerful pressure groups, defending, it says, the second amendment right of its 5.5 million members to bear arms. At any suggestion that those rights are under threat, the NRA sends its members out on to the streets in protest. In 2012, for example, NRA protestors mounted strong defences of gun ownership in the public and political outcry following the Sandy Hook Elementary School shooting, which claimed 26 victims – 20 of them aged just six or seven. The NRA even claimed that this tragedy – and many of the more than 230 school shootings that have taken place since the Columbine High School attack in 1999 – could have been prevented by having more guns in play, specifically by hiring armed guards to patrol America's educational establishments.

The NRA does not encourage this form of pushback only to remind America's government of its opposition to arms regulation, come what may. It also does it to win new members and generate funding, for it is a sad fact that every mass shooting or terrorist attack on American soil results in a spike in gun sales, NRA sign-ups and donations to the association.

Badge of honour: an NRA life membership patch, designed to be sewn on to a jacket or shirt.

As well as serving the needs of its individual members, the NRA also represents the interests of the gun-making industry. Arms manufacturers such as Smith & Wesson, Glock, Beretta, USA Midway and SIG Sauer are all generous funders of the NRA. What this means in practice is that the NRA has a strong vested interest in not just encouraging Americans to keep their guns but to buy more of them. For every gun that the Brazilian weapon manufacturer Taurus sells in America, for example, it purchases one NRA membership in return. Crimson Trace, a company that makes gun laser sighting equipment, donates 10 per cent of its profits to the NRA. Since 2005 the NRA has received more than US$50 million from gun manufacturers.

What the NRA does with its members' and gun-makers' money is where its deep state power is truly felt. As a major lobby group, the NRA is well placed to influence the political decision-making process. Politicians are carefully scrutinized for their support of second amendment issues and are rated on a scale of A to F accordingly. A-rated Republicans and Democrats receive sizeable NRA campaign funds, while those classed as B through to E get progressively less. F-rated politicians get nothing. During and since the presidency of Barack Obama, as American politics has become more polarized, the number of A-rated Democrats in Congress has fallen from 63 in 2008 to just three following the 2018 mid-term elections. This means that the NRA has become ever-more closely tied to the Republican Party, and, since 2016, its leader Donald Trump.

This is why the NRA became embroiled in the Mueller investigation, launched in 2017 to explore allegations that Russia influenced the presidential election of 2016 in order to get Donald Trump elected. In short, the NRA was accused of allowing its status as a registered charity to be exploited by Russian agents who used it to funnel dark money into the Trump campaign. Although the NRA at first denied this, the association's complicity was confirmed by a 2019 Senate Finance Committee report which found it had acted as a 'foreign asset' for Russia. When faced with the report, the NRA admitted taking Russian money but claimed that none of the cash was used for political purposes. Regardless of what happened to the Russian-sourced NRA cash, on becoming president Donald Trump in 2017 made great public show of supporting a new NRA-backed law overturning individual states' rights to prevent citizens carrying concealed weapons in public.

Rewriting the laws of the land

When it comes to new laws and regulations that promote their interests, corporate deep states are increasingly writing the legislation themselves through what are known as model bills. Analysis by *The Arizona Republic* newspaper and the Center for Public Integrity (CPI) in 2019 found that so-called 'copy and paste' bills, usually with the aim of protecting corporate interest against the public good, were being submitted to local legislatures from state to state containing exactly the same wording, with only regional details changed. The 2012 Asbestos Transparency Act, for example, did not quite live up to its name and was authored on behalf of the American asbestos industry. Among its terms was a limitation on the public's right to sue asbestos manufacturers for health conditions caused by the substance and a cap on the amount of damages consumers could claim.

As of 2020, the Asbestos Transparency Act has become law in 12 American states. It was written, like thousands of other model bills, by an organization called ALEC (the American Legislative Exchange Council). After drafting a model bill for a corporate client, ALEC will call on friendly councillors in state legislatures to introduce the law under their own name, earning them the undying gratitude of the business in question. Koch Industries is an avid model bill user, as are Exxon Mobil, Procter & Gamble, Molson Coors and many more. The energy company Enron sponsored model bills advocating electricity deregulation in the early 2000s, the results of which allowed it to perpetrate the fraudulent activity that led to it running up losses of more than US$60 billion. The *Arizona Republic*/CPI reporting found that 10,000 model bills had been introduced since 2001, with 4,301 on behalf of business, 4,012 representing conservative and Christian organizations, and 1,602 for liberal groups. To date, 20 per cent of these bills have been passed into law.

The Arlington, Virginia, headquarters of the conservative-minded model bill 'factory' the American Legislative Exchange Council (ALEC).

213

Introducing business-friendly legislation is one half of the corporate deep-state legal affairs equation; appointing receptive judges to approve that legislation is the other. At the end of the 1980s, a young Republican activist in Texas named Karl Rove pioneered a method of reconfiguring his state's Supreme Court by matching up corporations with ambitious, up-and-coming conservative judges, using Texas' chamber of commerce to launder dark money campaign funding to see liberal judges voted out of office and right-wingers voted in. 'The cases all started getting decided anti-consumer, on the side of big business,' said one retired Democrat judge. By the end of the 1990s corporate defendants in business malfeasance trials in Texas were victorious in up to 70 per cent of cases. Since the turn of the millennium, business interests including Home Depot, Wal-Mart and the insurer AIG have spent more than US$100 million in dark money attempting to instal explicitly pro-business judges into local legislatures and state Supreme Courts across America.

Koch Industries, always an innovator, took this approach one step further, using front organizations such as the pressure group Oklahomans for Judicial Excellence to publicly 'name and shame' liberal or supposedly anti-business judges in an effort to influence their future decision-making in a more corporate-friendly direction. Meanwhile, the company hired out five-star beach resorts and exclusive golf clubs to host all-expenses-paid legal seminars attended by known conservative judges, a tactic also employed by Shell and Exxon Mobil, among others.

The media and the message

Having secured political and legal support for their interests, the final way corporate deep states enjoy success is by influencing public opinion through the use of think tanks and the media.

Think tanks are effective fronts for recycling corporate deep state agendas into received wisdom – especially when they have been set up or funded by the corporations themselves. The Cato

Institute, for example, is one of America's most influential right-wing think tanks and produces a regular supply of carefully written academic reports extolling the virtues of the free market. Rarely in its papers' footnotes and references will you find any mention that the Cato Institute was co-founded by Charles Koch and is funded by him. The American Enterprise Institute, a think tank at the forefront of climate change denial studies, is also Koch-funded, along with the oil industry-friendly Heartland Institute, which also includes Exxon Mobil among its benefactors. Koch money has also found its way into the Heritage Foundation, a free-market, neo-conservative policy study organization founded by the Coors brewing family in 1973. Its current supporters include the major cigarette manufacturer Altria.

When it comes to propagating the findings of think tanks, or promoting their concerns more generally, the corporate deep states have extensive media interests to call on. Fox News is openly Republican and has developed an especially close relationship with Donald Trump, whose unashamed populism and controversy-ridden presidency perfectly suits the station's news-as-entertainment ethos. However, like Charles Koch, Fox's proprietor Rupert Murdoch is a right-wing libertarian with an absolute belief in the free market and from time to time a need is felt to remind the ideologically suspect president that the channel's support is not unconditional. This was the case in late 2019, as Donald Trump's impeachment trial got underway, coinciding with his widely criticized decision to abandon America's Kurdish allies in Syria. Fox News anchors and pundits began to openly criticize Donald Trump, something previously unthinkable. This was interpreted at the time as Fox/Murdoch warning the president to rein in his more divisive impulses with a general election just a year away and the threat of a Democrat victory all too real.

While Fox News openly displays its colours, other media organizations have a more underground influence on America's political life. Owned by the publicity-shy Smith family of

Baltimore, the Sinclair Broadcast Group runs 173 local TV stations across America and uses them to propagate a conservative belief system to around 40 per cent of the population. Following the 9/11 attacks, for example, the Smiths ordered all Sinclair TV stations to broadcast prepared editorials praising President George W. Bush's response to the al-Qaeda atrocity. When staff at Sinclair's WBFF channel in Baltimore complained that this compromised the station's political objectivity they were overruled. In April 2017 another Smith directive required every Sinclair channel to air – nine times a week – a 10-minute op-ed slot called *Bottom Line with Boris* by a newly hired pundit, Boris Epshteyn. As Epshteyn was Donald Trump's former assistant communications director, this was interpreted by media watchers as an attempt to curry favour with the president, especially as Epshteyn's slavishly pro-Trump monologues led one commentator to label his show 'industrial strength propaganda'.

The same year that it hired Epshteyn, Sinclair successfully lobbied his former boss to relax media ownership rules so that it could purchase for US$3.9 billion an extra 42 TV stations to add to its portfolio. The president's generosity was not unexpected. The Smiths had been major Trump donors during the 2016 election and he had appeared on Sinclair news and discussion shows 15 times during the presidential campaign, often in crucial swing states; Trump's opponent, Hillary Clinton, did not appear once. Although the Sinclair TV purchase eventually fell through, the manner in which approval for the deal was secured was straight out of the deep-state playbook.

Away from the world of TV, the little-known Meredith Corporation is a powerful conservative print media group exerting a more underground, but no less important, deep-state influence. This came to light in 2017, when the Iowa-based publisher paid US$2.8 billion for Time Inc., home of the iconic news and current affairs title *Time*, as well as *Sports Illustrated* and *People* magazines. Commentators wondered why the company behind folksy American

Headquarters of the Sinclair Broadcast Group in Hunt Valley, Maryland.

fare such as *American Patchwork & Quilting*, *FamilyFun* and *Midwest Living* was interested in owning one of the great liberal titles of modern times. The plot thickened when it was revealed the deal had been facilitated by a US$650 million investment by Koch Equity Development (KED), the private equity subsidiary of Koch Industries. Charles Koch was quick to reassure the world that his was a purely business investment and that he had no intention of interfering in the editorial position of *Time* in any way.

In almost every media profile of Charles Koch, he is portrayed as a cold-eyed, ruthless operator, unflinchingly true to his libertarian, market-based beliefs. However, once the Time Inc. purchase was complete a curious thing began to happen. In *Time* magazine (and in virtually no other centrist publication) a different picture of the multi-billionaire emerged. 'Charles Koch Is Known For Conservative Advocacy: A New Report Highlights His Charitable Giving', ran one *Time* headline in October 2018; 'Koch Network To Push For Legal Status For Dreamers' ran another *Time* story in January 2019, flagging up the mogul's pro-immigration credentials. A clue as to why the magazine was promoting this kinder, gentler version of its owners' benefactor came in June 2019, with another *Time* story titled 'Coming Soon To A Democratic Primary: Candidates Backed By Charles Koch'. With the 2020 presidential election just a year away, the Trump-led Republican Party was being reminded that Koch's support was not a given and that his free-market, anti-protectionist, deregulatory libertarian agenda needed to be incorporated into any re-election platform the president was putting together.

Aside from the PR opportunities it afforded, Koch's investment in Time Inc. and his financial backing of the Meredith Corporation had a deeper benefit. Both media organizations held valuable data on millions of subscribers and customers. On buying into both companies, Koch was able to access that information and run it through his data analytics agency i360 to produce incredibly detailed profiles for up to 250 million Americans to be used for voter targeting and advertising in a manner similar to that supposedly employed by Cambridge Analytica (see p.209).

ADMINISTRATIVE DEEP STATES

Following his inauguration as president in early 2017, Donald Trump immediately began to complain that his legislative agenda was being undermined by an insidious deep-state alliance of civil servants and security service establishment elites that runs the United States in a similar fashion to the old-boy network in the UK and the *grandes écoles* cadre of France (see pp.44–9). As we've seen, this is not quite the case. Much opposition to Trump has come from the right rather than the left, from conservative and libertarian corporate deep states such as Koch Industries. But there is little political capital to be gained by the president conceding that the powerful businesses that publicly support him are, on occasion, privately thwarting his plans.

That's not to say, however, that the civil service and the nation's security agencies do not have their own self-interests to protect. Let's look at how they have done this since the end of World War II, and how the presidential election of 2016 presented them with new challenges to navigate.

They work for you?

In the 19th century, America had no established civil service. Instead there was the so-called 'spoils system', whereby each incoming president brought in his own administrators, a state of affairs that opened up civil service posts to the highest bidder or the president's closest cronies. It was only after a disappointed office-seeker assassinated President Garfield in 1881 that the spoils system was abandoned and merit-based selection introduced instead. This worked well and was expanded significantly during the New Deal presidency of Franklin D. Roosevelt in 1933–45, meaning that America emerged from World War II with more bureaucrats than ever before. This alarmed some on the right who believed it smacked of impending socialism.

With the Soviet Union occupying half of Europe and leftist regimes establishing themselves in South America, especially Guatemala (see pp.145–51), America experienced a 'red scare' in the 1950s, where a deep state of communist agents and sympathizers was thought to be infiltrating the country. In 1938, the House Un-American Activities Committee (HUAC) had been established to investigate allegations of subversion and treasonous activity in public and private life, but by the early 1950s its main focus was on arresting the spread of communism. In 1950, the State Department official Alger Hiss was convicted of espionage allegations and this was followed in 1953 by the executions of the supposed Soviet spies Julius and Ethel Rosenberg. Although these were isolated incidents, in the public imagination they were the tip of the iceberg. The perception that the Soviets were planning world domination was intensified by the intervention of Joseph McCarthy, an unstable, alcoholic senator from Wisconsin. In 1950, likely to lose his seat in upcoming elections, McCarthy staged a popularity-boosting PR stunt by claiming he had obtained a list of 205 communists known to be working at the State Department. Although the list was a complete fabrication, it put the senator on the national stage.

For the next four years McCarthy presented himself as the scourge of communism, grilling scores of government officials and even figures from the entertainment industry in public hearings that ruined the careers of many innocent individuals. In the meantime, America's rulers succumbed to a form of collective madness as they unquestioningly approved McCarthy's every wrong move. In 1950 Congress approved the McCarthy-inspired McCarran Internal Security Act, which defined scores of liberal lobby groups as 'communist fronts' and also approved the establishment of concentration camps for alleged communists in times of national emergency. Four years later, Congress passed the McCarthy-influenced Communist Control Act, which condemned the American Communist Party and strongly recommended it be outlawed. But when, in 1954, McCarthy attacked the army for supposedly pro-Soviet bias he overstepped the mark. He was censured by his fellow senators and served out his remaining two years in political office shunned by many of the same men and women who had enthusiastically supported his crusade just months before.

Seventeen years after McCarthy's fall from grace, government bureaucracy was again accused of running its own deep-state conspiracy, this time against the sitting president, Richard Nixon. It began with the leaking of a top-secret government report on the progress of the war in Vietnam to the *New York Times* in 1971. The leaker was Daniel Ellsberg, a 40-year-old defence analyst and researcher who had helped to compile the so-called 'Pentagon Papers' and who in doing so became opposed to America's involvement in the conflict. Although Ellsberg acted on his own initiative, for Nixon, a man with something of a persecution complex, the leaking of the Pentagon Papers was evidence of an establishment plot against him. 'Down in the government are a bunch of sons of bitches,' he told his cabinet. 'Many who sit in the meetings and debriefings . . . are out to get us.' In another tirade to aides he declared, 'We're up against an enemy, a conspiracy. They're using any means. We are going to use any means. Is that clear?' Among those means he used was an attempt to gather incriminating evidence against Nixon's deep-state enemies, which meant authorizing an illegal break-in at the Democratic National Committee headquarters in Washington D.C.'s Watergate building on 17 June 1972. When the burglars were caught red-handed, Nixon engaged in a botched cover-up that ultimately led to his resignation in 1974.

According to some, Richard Nixon's paranoia and Joseph McCarthy's attacks on government officials and civil servants are among the inspirations behind Donald Trump's complaints against the 'deep state' he claims is out to get him. The wall between America and Mexico that he campaigned so vigorously for remained unbuilt, he said, because the bureaucrats blocked it; the repeal of Obamacare was obstructed by liberals in the civil service. As for supposed Russian interference in the 2016 election, in Trump's narrative it's a vast conspiracy by sore losers still pining for Hillary Clinton, cooked up by the Democrats and their deep-state allies in the establishment, which led to the unsuccessful attempt to impeach him at the end of 2019.

In some respects, the Democrats' efforts to impeach Donald Trump was actually a blessing for the president. It allowed Trump to tie his Republican senators and representatives closer to him than ever before, and it was common on American television news and comments programmes at the time to see political figures on the right making public declarations of loyalty to their leader and denouncing the 'witch hunt' against him. It also served to rouse the more extreme elements of Trump's base to action, reaffirming any flagging faith they may have had in him. It was QAnon all over again, some said, evoking the right-wing conspiracy theory first touted in 2017 by an anonymous source online, claiming to have access to classified documents proving the Democrats, the FBI and government officials were trying to bring down the president. This in turn reminded many in Trump's base of the linked 'Pizzagate' scandal, a bizarre but widely circulated rumour spread just before the 2016 election that Hillary Clinton and other prominent Democrats were involved in a child sex ring run out of a Washington pizza parlour and bowling alley.

KEEPING AMERICANS SAFE

If the idea of a malicious administrative deep state seems fanciful, it's more plausible to imagine that America's security services pursue their own, sometimes hidden, agendas. Organizations such as the FBI and CIA are by nature secretive and it is often in the government's interests not to know the full extent of their activities so that plausible deniability can be claimed when particularly controversial operations go wrong.

We've already met the Dulles brothers, whose post-war mandate to the CIA to advance America's interests around the globe, especially against the Soviet Union, sealed its reputation as an organization willing to act with former Nazis, political usurpers, terrorist groups and dictators in order to achieve its aims. But, discounting instances where both the CIA and the FBI have exceeded their remit in what could be described as an excess of zeal, and putting to one side the CIA's as-yet unproven involvement in the assassination of President John F. Kennedy in 1963, it is difficult to describe many of their actions as undeniably deep state.

One notable exception was the Iran-Contra scandal of 1985. This developed when it was revealed that the administration of President Ronald Reagan had broken an international arms embargo to illegally sell weapons to its sworn enemy, Iran, in that country's long-running war with its neighbour, Iraq (which the US was openly supporting and funding at the time). When this illicit deal came to light, America had already sold 1,500 missiles to Iran for US$30 million. The arms deal was arranged not purely for money but also in return for Iranian help freeing US hostages held by Iran-backed Hezbollah fighters in Lebanon. However, with US$30 million going begging, the National Security Agency (NSA) – of which more later – was tasked with diverting the payments to right-wing drug-trafficking rebels in Nicaragua known as Contras who were attempting to bring down the country's socialist Sandinista government. The key figure in the affair was an NSA officer called Lt. Col. Oliver North, who in an explosive, and televised, Congressional hearing testimony in 1987 revealed the workings of the Iran-Contra deal and told his questioners he believed that President Reagan was fully aware of the operation – a claim Reagan at first denied then later admitted.

Although the Iran-Contra affair was illegal and unsavoury, it was not, strictly speaking, a deep-state action. But what came after was. When the arms deal was done, the Iranians were instructed to pay the US$30 million fee into the Luxembourg-registered Bank of Credit & Commerce International (BCCI). This was an institution known in intelligence circles as the 'bank of crooks and criminals', and after it went into liquidation in 1991 investigations turned up intriguing evidence that the BCCI may well have been a front organization part-owned and operated by the CIA, which used parts of the funds deposited in it to run off-the-books black-ops not sanctioned by the US government. BCCI-funded activity carried out by the CIA was said to have included money laundering, arms sales, terrorism sponsorship, drug-trafficking, gold smuggling and other nefarious activities collectively known as 'the black network'. Even today, the CIA's activities with the BCCI remain unclear – proof, perhaps, that it was one of the agency's more successful deep-state enterprises.

America's biggest secret of all

The NSA's role in the Iran-Contra affair was a rare example of it being exposed to public scrutiny. Established in 1952, the NSA's primary role was, and still is, the collection and processing of all forms of radio, telephone, electrical and digital communication at home and abroad. But over time the organization has stealthily built up its power base at the expense of its more famous siblings, the FBI and the CIA. Today, the NSA has the biggest budget and the most personnel of all 17 of America's intelligence agencies and its power keeps on growing, along with its tendency to act independently of any official oversight.

The source of the NSA's growth has been the huge expansion of the internet, the digital world and mobile phone telephony since the 1990s. It's the NSA's job to monitor every US-based phone call, email, credit card transaction, text, tweet, Instagram communication and Facebook post, all day, every day. It has infiltrated media giants such as Google and Yahoo, not always legally, and processes around two billion communications each year. It has listening posts in every US embassy and consulate and has bugged those of many other nations. This short summary of the NSA's work is only a fraction of its activities, and we know what we know because of the whistleblower and former NSA contractor Edward Snowden (see pp.245–6).

So secretive is the NSA that it's not known how many people work there. It's thought to have 35,000–55,000 employees, but it also oversees an empire of private firms and operatives that could account for up to 500,000 people. With an US$11 billion budget behind it, the NSA is virtually a small nation: a national security state. As we'll see in the next chapter, the NSA frequently conducts illegal wiretapping operations and goes way beyond its government-sanctioned mandate as regards who and how it monitors.

Since the 2016 presidential election, relations between the intelligence services and the White House have been strained, to say the least. In doing its job of investigating possible pro-Trump interference by Russia into the presidential campaign, the FBI in particular has incurred Donald Trump's displeasure. He fired the FBI's director James Comey in May 2017 and dismissed his

Black box recorder: the high-tech, top-secret National Security Agency (NSA) HQ in Fort Meade, Maryland.

replacement, acting director Andrew McCabe, just a few months later. In one version of events, both men were part of the liberal deep-state plot to oust Trump in a coup; in another version, they were collateral damage in the president's fight to hide the true story of how he was elected leader of the free world at the behest of Russia's Vladimir Putin.

Russia's role or otherwise in the 2016 election is a subject of some dispute (see pp.246–8). What is clear, however, is that the USA, by virtue of its wealth, power and politics, is particularly susceptible to a multiplicity of deep-state interests so deeply embedded that they may be impossible to remove.

CHAPTER 9
DIGITAL DEEP STATES

ALTHOUGH IT'S ONLY been an integral part of our daily lives since the early 2000s, it's impossible to imagine life without its digital dimension today. Our smartphones and computers are the means by which we communicate, how we find out things about the world. They show us what to think and, if some scientific studies are correct, are changing how we think too.

The technology is developing so quickly it's proving impossible for laws and accepted moral norms to keep pace, leaving an ethical gap we are struggling to bridge. This is good news for those who make or own big tech, or who best understand how to profit from its possibilities. This chapter looks at how the digital revolution happened and the corporations that have grown to amass enormous power from it, by fair means and foul. Then we'll see how bad actors are using the digital space to influence the social and political choices we make, specifically in the US presidential election and the Brexit referendum of 2016. Finally, we'll investigate what three of the cyberworld's most active nation states are doing to carve out their own zones of influence in the virtual sphere.

CORPORATE DIGITAL DEEP STATES

Microsoft, Apple, Google, Amazon and Facebook are the five big tech corporations that have the longest reach and the biggest global influence today. Their collective histories are those of the internet and the development of digital culture itself, including its incredible achievements and its serious missteps. This takes in underhand and sometimes illegal activity in pursuit of more customers, more users, more data and more profits. Part of this comes from a lack of oversight from lawmakers and politicians, who often do not understand exactly what it is these companies do and have usually been content to let them regulate themselves. In recent years, following allegations of wrongdoing and abuse of power, attempts have been made to rein in the influence of big tech. But is it too late? In this section we'll see how tech got to be big, and whether it's now bigger than the governments that in theory control it.

ARPANET and Microsoft: where it all began

Every computer buff knows that the internet and email in their earliest forms grew out of a Cold War US Department of Defense programme to create information-sharing and communication systems for the military and intelligence services that could survive a nuclear attack on the United States by the Soviet Union. This early network was known as ARPANET (Advanced Research Projects Agency Network) and it went live in 1969.

It would be another 20 years before anyone outside the Pentagon could benefit from the technology that created ARPANET. That moment came in 1989, when a British computer scientist called Tim Berners-Lee based at the CERN nuclear research institute in Switzerland developed an ARPANET-style research program he called the World Wide Web, and what we today call the internet. In the two decades between ARPANET and the launch of the World Wide Web, a huge explosion in home and business computing created hundreds of millions of users now able to contact each other instantly through email and with a resource that, potentially, made all human knowledge available. Some at the time urged caution – and regulation – when dealing with this new virtual world, but they were largely disregarded as humankind swiftly embraced the new reality. We are still dealing with the implications of this today, as we live through a digital revolution happening in hyper-real time.

The rise of Microsoft

America's first tech entrepreneurs made their names in northern California, emerging from the area's post-hippy counterculture and building in ideas of freedom and anti-authoritarian libertarianism from the start. Steve Jobs and Steve Wozniak, for example, who founded Apple in 1976, typified the generation of long-haired and bearded young men (there were few women) who held 'straight' tech jobs by day but at night congregated in places such as the Homebrew Computer Club in Menlo Park in San Francisco's Bay area, developing their hacking skills, building their own computers and perfecting the art of 'phreaking', the illegal accessing and reconfiguring of telecoms networks to give users unlimited and free phone calls worldwide.

The idea that large parts of the digital world should be free still obtains today, and it has had major implications on the development of how digital deep states work, as well as being a driving force behind many hacking groups and entities such as Wikipedia. But there is a commercial dimension, too, and it's a large one. When Bill Gates set up Microsoft in 1975, followed by Jobs' and Wozniak's Apple a year later, the budding entrepreneurs had to make a decision: incorporate their hacking and phreaking ideals into their new companies, or turn their businesses into proprietary corporations. With the home computer market growing exponentially throughout the 1980s and '90s and billions of dollars on offer, it was no contest.

Microsoft in particular had cornered the home personal computing (PC) software market early, leaving Apple, with its more expensive and higher-spec products, to be the brand of choice for more niche activities such as publishing and design. Microsoft was so dominant that it was the subject of numerous allegations of restrictive practices, which resulted in it being tried for operating as a monopoly in 1998. The case centred around Microsoft's struggles with its younger rival Netscape to control access to the newly emerging internet. In the early 1990s, Netscape had capitalized on the opening of the World Wide Web by quickly launching its Netscape Navigator browser and helping itself to 75 per cent of the market by 1994. Microsoft, eager to break into the online world, developed its own browser, Internet Explorer (IE), integrating it into the Windows operating system that virtually all PCs used at the time. By giving IE 'free' to all PC users, Microsoft ensured Netscape's paid-for Navigator never stood a chance. Today Netscape is seen as little more than a footnote in early internet history, a victim of the over-mighty Microsoft in the browser wars of the 1990s.

After a two-year trial, Judge Thomas P. Jackson ruled in April 2000 that Microsoft was indeed operating in a monopolistic manner and ordered the company to be broken up under the terms of the Sherman Anti-Trust Act (see p.182). It was not a decision the company took lying down. In 1998, when the trial began, the Democrat Bill Clinton was president. But with mid-term elections taking place that same year, the traditionally Democrat-supporting Microsoft changed tack and used its lobbying power to back Republican Party candidates instead, successfully ensuring the Grand Old Party kept its majorities in both houses of Congress and reducing the Democrat administration's ability to prosecute its case against Microsoft more vigorously. Although this slowed the legal process it did not stop it, and after Judge Jackson's decision Microsoft lodged an appeal and threw its weight behind the Republicans again in the 2000 presidential election, the party's candidate George W. Bush having publicly declared on the campaign trail he would not have approved the action against Microsoft and did not support breaking up the company.

Microsoft's office: the corporation's HQ, known as the Redmond Campus, close to Seattle.

Bush won the election and within a year, his administration came to an agreement with Microsoft. In return for allowing in theory non-Microsoft-created software to be used on Windows' operating systems, the company was allowed to remain intact. Having achieved the decision it wanted, Microsoft reverted to type and put 61 per cent of its political funding at the disposal of the Democrat Party in 2004. Yet this was not the end of Microsoft's brushes with the law: in 2013 EU regulators fined the company a record US$732 million for going back on its agreement to allow Windows users to download non-Microsoft web browsers more easily.

BIG TECH, BIG PROBLEMS

Microsoft's 2001 deal with the US government was seen at the time as a victory for the tech giant. It remained one and indivisible, after all. But it can also be seen as a moment when Bill Gates was forced to reluctantly open the door for other digital entrepreneurs to join the internet revolution. The result, according to contemporary pundits and legal experts, was going to be a huge increase in innovation and competition. In this, they were only half right. Since 2001 the digital world has seen one incredible technical development after another – and the narrowing of its 'ownership' to an increasingly small coterie of tycoons who, in an earlier age, would probably have been called robber barons (see pp.184–8).

Facebook, Amazon, Apple and Google (FAAG) are the four biggest 'heirs' of the Microsoft settlement. Acting individually and sometimes in concert too, they are writing the book on how big tech determines what the digital world is and what it can be. In the process they are reshaping society, in large part free of political control or oversight, and where attempts are made to regulate them they usually have the resources and the deep-state power to go their own way.

Facebook's anti-social media

In 2019, Facebook's revenues were US$70.7 billion and its market value US$520 billion. As the platform is free to use, the vast majority of its income – almost 72 per cent – derives from advertisers hungry for the data of Facebook's 2.5 billion users, one-third of the world's population. What happens to that data is a source of some controversy and will be examined in greater detail on pp.241–2. Here we'll focus on how Facebook uses its wealth and power to manage competition and buy political influence.

As the world's pre-eminent social network, Facebook deals with potential rivals by reaching for its wallet. A master of the defensive acquisition, Facebook employed this strategy in 2012, when it picked up the photo-based platform Instagram for US$1 billion (it's worth US$100 billion today) and the message-based mobile application WhatsApp in 2014 for US$19 billion. Allowing brands such as the younger-profiling Instagram to remain in operation gives Facebook access to new markets, but just as importantly it creates the illusion of competition. Three very large social media platforms look a lot less like a monopoly than one enormous one.

When questions are asked about Facebook's dominant position the company is ready to deal with them. In 2019 it spent US$16.7 million on lobbying, more than any other tech giant, and retained 71 lobbyists – 66 of whom were revolvers (see p.201). In March 2019 the *Guardian* newspaper and *Computer Weekly* magazine acquired a Facebook memo that revealed how the organization exerted political influence, making it clear to countries including India, Vietnam, Argentina, Brazil and Malaysia that it would withhold investment in their economies unless they supported or passed Facebook-friendly laws. Canada's government was told a new Facebook data centre would be relocated if local jurisdictional disputes were not resolved in the company's favour – and they duly were. In Europe, Facebook lobbied the EU to tone down data usage protocols in the proposed General Data Protection Regulation (GDPR) provisions that came into effect in May 2018. Specifically, the memo appeared to show Facebook targeting then-Irish prime minister Enda Kenny as a proxy for its anti-GDPR activities, pointing out that Facebook's European HQ was based in Dublin and it employed hundreds of locals. With the company a major investor in the Irish economy, Kenny was described as a 'friend of Facebook' who, with Ireland due to take over the EU presidency, would be in a position to 'influence the European Data Directive decisions'. The Cambridge academic and digital technology expert John Naughton told the *Guardian* this amounted to little more than Ireland's 'vassalage' to Facebook, a company he described as a 'data monster'. The memo also claimed that Kenny offered to use the 'significant influence' of the EU presidency in Facebook's favour, an allegation Kenny denied.

The leaked memo also named the UK's then chancellor of the exchequer George Osborne as a potential ally in its GDPR fight, claiming he had a meeting with Facebook CEO Sheryl Sandberg at the World Economic Forum in Davos to discuss the matter, telling her he would 'figure out how to get more involved'. Then, in October 2018, Facebook surprised the business and political worlds by unveiling Nick Clegg, the UK's former deputy prime minister, as its new vice-president of global affairs and communications. Clegg said he was taking the PR and lobbying role because he was 'convinced that the culture was changing' in the company following allegations of data misuse and Facebook-facilitated Russian interference in the US presidential election and UK Brexit referendum of 2016. At a technology conference in January 2020, Clegg told his audience: 'We are getting better and better at protecting elections from foreign interference.' However, this did not quite square with the official view in Westminster when, in March 2020, Conservative ministers in Britain were told to change the official government line that there were 'no successful examples' of Russian interference in recent British national votes, embracing both the Brexit referendum and the December 2019 general election. This implied that Facebook and other social media platforms remained open to abuse almost four years after the scandals of 2016 and their promises to improve.

Google: doing the right thing?

The big winner in the browser wars of the 1990s was Google. While Netscape and Microsoft fought it out, in 1998 two tech entrepreneurs named Larry Page and Sergey Brin created a browser whose simple, uncluttered interface was easy to use and whose technology returned search results quickly and in greater volume than its rivals. It was a massive hit and soon made Google the world's most popular search engine.

Today, Google has expanded well beyond its search-engine operations. Through its parent company Alphabet, it embraces

Sir Nick Clegg, former UK deputy prime minister and, since 2018, Facebook's high-profile PR man.

multiple companies and services. As well as owning how we search the internet, it oversees how 1.5 billion Gmail users communicate with each other and what 2 billion YouTube viewers watch. Crucially, it owns and runs the Android operating system that powers 2.5 billion phone devices worldwide; on top of that it also owns Google Play, the download centre that determines which apps and games Android phones and devices can use. Ownership of Google Play allows the company to rank its products above competitors' and remove rival apps with little or no notice and for any reason. Google can preference its products on its search engine, too, a practice for which it was cited by the EU in 2016. A year later, a *Wall Street Journal* investigation revealed that Google was still at it, reporting how searches for items such as laptops and phones returned Google-related products in the site's top-ranked paid search slots in 91 per cent of attempts.

Every move you make on Google is monitored, registered and remembered. This means that the company has incredibly detailed data on every phone call, text, email, journey, YouTube view, search and purchase you make. How Google uses that data, for itself and as a product to sell to third parties, has landed the company in regulatory trouble several times. In 2012 Google was fined US$22.5 million by US regulators for failing to tighten up its data-mining practices – a figure that was dwarfed by the €2.42 billion, €4.34 billion and €1.49 billion fines handed out to it by the EU for abuse of power offences in 2017, 2018 and 2019. Back in the US, in September 2019 Google settled a US$170 million claim with the FTC (Federal Trade Commission) over claims that Google-owned YouTube had knowingly and illegally collected personal information on pre-adolescent viewers and sold the data to advertisers. Privacy campaigners complained the fine was a drop in the ocean, and that no individuals at Google or YouTube were prosecuted or censured. With annual revenues of US$132.2 billion in 2019, Google is easily able to absorb any fine imposed upon it, and with almost 63 per cent of its income derived from search engine advertising and 16 per cent from YouTube advertising it has little reason to end its policy of asking for forgiveness rather than seeking permission when it comes to data misuse allegations.

This may be one of the reasons why Google has slashed its lobbying budget in recent years, almost halving it to US$12 million in 2019, for example, and firing half of its 103 lobbyists. Like Apple (see pp.238–40) Google is cutting out the middleman and going straight to the top where possible in its pursuit of political leverage. This is especially the case in Europe, where Google has been on the end of some major fines in the late 2010s, leading the company to make high-ranking UK hires from Downing Street, the Home Office, the Treasury, the Department for Education and the Department for Transport to extend its influence. Google has been adept at getting its people into politics, too. In 2016, British prime minister Theresa May appointed Baroness Joanna Shields, a former Google managing director, as her minister for internet safety, and a few years earlier David Cameron appointed Google's executive chairman Eric Schmidt to his business advisory council.

Amazon's uncharted waters

The digital world's biggest department store, Amazon really does have something for everyone. Small wonder then that its founder, Jeff Bezos, is the world's richest man, worth an estimated US$150 billion in 2019. As for his company, it earned US$278.8 billion that same year, and was valued at US$873.4 billion.

Almost half of all e-commerce goes through Amazon, from both self-generated and third-party sales, and this can leave vendors vulnerable to the company's predatory instincts. For example, it is not unheard of for Amazon to replicate the goods of smaller companies and sell them under its own brand names at cheaper prices. It was only in 2019 that Amazon in the US reluctantly lifted a long-running restriction forbidding third-party vendors from selling their goods cheaper elsewhere, a policy it had been forced to abandon in Europe in 2013. While this was good news for smaller rivals, in practical terms it's not in their interests to undercut a company that can arbitrarily bar any seller from its site if it falls out with them.

As important as e-commerce is to Amazon, the company is also growing two more of its digital businesses: Amazon Web Services (AWS) and online advertising. AWS is a major player in cloud-based data storage and controls one-third of the market, making it larger than the possibly better-known Google Cloud and Microsoft's Azure. So rapid was AWS' growth in the 2010s that in late 2019 the FTC began investigating Amazon over claims that it pressurized potential business partners to use its cloud service if they wanted to work with the company in other areas. At the time of writing this probe is still ongoing. Regarding online advertising, Amazon has a competitive advantage over fellow 'data monsters' Facebook and Google in that it has very detailed information on

Amazon founder and the world's richest man, Jeff Bezos.

the shopping histories of its customers. These are details marketers and advertisers pay premium prices to acquire.

In 2019, Amazon spent US$16.7 million on lobbying and sought to influence Washington's legislators on more issues that any of its rivals. Among its lobbyists is Jay Carney, Barack Obama's former press secretary and a well-connected D.C. insider. Carney is one of more than 100 Amazon lobbyists, 74 per cent of whom are revolvers. In addition, Jeff Bezos spends a lot of time in Washington himself and is a regular attendee at prestigious black-tie events alongside establishment grandees such as the super-investor Warren Buffet and Allan Greenspan, former chairman of the Federal Reserve Bank. Bezos' high-level networking is part of a concerted strategy for Amazon to land lucrative government contracts to store civil and military archives in the cloud. In 2018 Amazon was in line to win a US$10 billion Pentagon cloud contract known as 'Jedi', only to be thwarted at the last minute by complaints from IBM, Oracle and Microsoft that Amazon had developed an improper relationship with a former Pentagon decision-maker during the bidding process. Although Microsoft eventually won the contract, Amazon, with its powerful army of Washington lobbyists, was able in March 2020 to get the Department of Defense to reconsider its award of 'Jedi' to Microsoft and Jeff Bezos may yet prevail in this fight.

At the same time as trying to land 'Jedi', Amazon was also pitching to host a US$50 billion government e-commerce portal which, if successful, would make Jeff Bezos America's official office supplier. When an alliance of suppliers called the Information Technology Industry Council (ITI) opposed Amazon's bid, the company hit back by effectively taking over the ITI and then forming a separate trade association of its own called the Alliance for Digital Innovation (ADI), a consortium of at least 19 Amazon-linked cloud-based companies which pointedly excluded Microsoft, Google, IBM and Oracle – Amazon's biggest Washington competitors.

The fly in the ointment to Amazon's ambitions since 2016 has been the antipathy between President Donald Trump and Jeff Bezos. This is in part motivated by Bezos' ownership of the *Washington Post*, which has been critical of Trump's administration but which Bezos says remains editorially independent from him. However, this is only a minor issue for the company. Amazon has longer-term concerns than the Trump presidency, and if it succeeds in its 'Jedi' and government e-commerce ambitions its deep-state efforts will have helped the company become firmly integrated into the legitimate state itself as the keeper of some of America's most sensitive civil and military secrets.

Apple comes home

In operation since 1976, Apple is now one of the wise elders of the digital world. Unlike most of its rivals, it derives the vast majority of its revenue from the manufacture of hardware, mainly iPhones, but also iPads and computers. Globally, iPhones account for just under 23 per cent of the mobile market – but as the average price for an iPhone is around US$800, against an average Android cost of US$500, the profit gap is not as wide as it first seems. This, along with Apple's venerable status and history of innovation and reinvention, is the reason why its market capitalization in 2019 was US$1.09 trillion, higher than any of its rivals, and its revenue was US$259 billion.

Apple's control of its hardware is tight (literally so, as its devices are famously difficult to unseal). But when it comes to software its grip is less secure, which has led it to engage in questionable practices to protect its position. The Apple-controlled App Store accounted for US$16 billion of the company's revenue in 2019 and it's a profitable market other app developers need to have a presence on. To gain this, they must pay Apple a 30 per cent commission for every download purchased, a high rate that in June 2019 led a group of developers to file a lawsuit against the company for acting as an 'abusive monopoly'. This commission, they and unhappy App Store users complained, forced them to increase their prices to offset the Apple 'tax'. The Supreme Court in America agreed, ruling in 2019 that App Store customers could sue Apple for driving up the cost of products on its site.

On the subject of tax, Apple's fiscal arrangements have not been without controversy. For several years, from 2004 to at least 2014, the California-based company kept its money elsewhere, employing a complicated accounting technique dubbed 'Double Irish with a Dutch Sandwich' that routed cash through Irish subsidiaries and Holland and then on to the Caribbean. By 2004, one third of Apple's revenues was held in Ireland. The company paid as little as 2.2 per cent tax on foreign profits in this way. By the early 2010s it was paying barely any tax in large areas of its business.

A US Senate report from 2013 revealed that the Irish business that ran Apple's operations in Europe had no employees, and was therefore a shell company. This was followed in 2016 by the EU competition commissioner claiming that Apple had received 'illegal state aid' from Ireland and fined the company €13 billion, the largest corporate tax fine ever. Interestingly, the Irish government sided with Apple in this case, not wanting to see the company take its revenues elsewhere. Apple and the Republic of Ireland thereafter ditched the 'Double Irish' setup and replaced it with something called the CAIA arrangement, which saw US$300 billion of Apple cash remain safely stored in the Emerald Isle. The Nobel laureate Paul Krugman called this financial sleight of hand 'Leprechaun Economics'.

This all changed in 2018, following Donald Trump's controversial tax reforms (see pp.206–7), after which Apple repatriated many of its offshore funds, signing a cheque for a cut-price US$38 billion in outstanding taxes to the US Treasury in the process. Apple's 'homecoming' was the result of two years of careful political discussions between Tim Cook, the company's CEO, and Donald Trump himself. Cleverly playing on the president's populist and nationalist instincts, Cook persuaded Trump that Apple's injection of more than US$300 billion into the US economy would be a big political win and that he was prepared to leave Ireland in return for preferential tax breaks. Trump was also able to bask in Cook's claim that, since becoming president, Apple had increased its US 'job footprint' to 2.4 million workers (in reality it employs around 130,000 people in America).

By playing the role of flattering courtier, Tim Cook got everything he needed from Donald Trump, extracting his company from a tricky situation and winning the president's favour in the process. Of all the big tech bosses, Tim Cook is very much the apple of Trump's eye.

From new robber barons to Bond villains

Microsoft, Facebook, Google, Amazon and Apple are the Standard Oils and J.P. Morgans of the digital age, giant corporations that emerged from the pack in a dynamic era of unparalleled innovation and woke up one morning to find themselves in charge of everything – unofficially, at least.

Governments – and government regulators – have struggled to keep up with the rate of technological change that big tech companies have driven, and the tools at their disposal are generally not enough to keep the companies in line. The people who run the digital giants know this, so there is little incentive for them to change what they do if the risks involved are not greater than the rewards for poor business practices. Company owners, managers and executives are never held personally responsible for wrongdoing, so even if they get caught breaking the rules, individuals know they can hide behind their corporate firewalls for protection. Furthermore, the fines levied against misbehaving tech corporations are simply too small to have behaviour-changing effects, especially when teams of expert lawyers deliberately spin out appeals processes and use stalling tactics to ensure that cases drag on for years or sometimes get 'forgotten about' when new elected officials take office with closer ties to the big tech companies than their predecessors.

As they grow, the big tech firms stifle competition and innovation by driving new companies out of the marketplace. Venture capitalists are reluctant to invest in promising start-ups if they think the companies they nurture will be bought out or closed down by larger rivals. Apple, Amazon and Google have gained unfair advantages by owning commercial platforms where they ensure their products always have pride of place.

Yet as much as the digital giants compete with each other, they also collude when it is to their mutual benefit, acting like the cartels America's anti-trust law is designed to prohibit. In late 2018, the *New York Times* gained access to internal Facebook documents showing how, even as it was embroiled in the post-2016 Russia probe scandal, the company exempted other tech firms from its privacy rules and gave them detailed access to its users' data. Microsoft's Bing search engine was allowed to see the names of almost all Facebook users' friends without consent, and Netflix and Spotify were allowed to read Facebook users' private messages. Amazon and Yahoo were also given privileged user information.

So, why do governments and regulators look the other way or soft pedal on fines and punishments when big tech goes bad? The answer, like most things, is the bottom line. Collectively, the tech firms have converted many of their assets into US$1 trillion held in offshore corporate bond accounts. This is the financial equivalent of ransomware, as it means the companies can threaten to dump the bonds when the subject of regulation or meaningful Anti-Trust legislation is raised against them, an act that could force the financial markets to crash and that no government would allow to happen. In this way the big tech firms have made themselves too big to control.

RUNNING INTERFERENCE

One aspect of Donald Trump's election strategy in 2016 that worked particularly well was his digital campaign. A large part of this was the use of Facebook to send highly targeted ads and posts to tens of millions of Americans to persuade them to vote for Trump or not to vote for his Democrat rival, Hillary Clinton. When analysts looked into the Trump campaign's Facebook activity it soon became apparent something unusual had gone on. This is not the place to rehearse the finer details of the Cambridge Analytica (CA) affair, because in deep-state terms the question is not so much what CA did but how much Facebook knew about it. Nothing at all, Facebook's founder and CEO Mark Zuckerberg claimed when he faced questions on the matter before Congress in April 2018. Facebook's user agreements needed tightening, he confessed, having been found wanting when targeted by bad actors; his users' data was sacred, and he admitted that Facebook had failed to protect it.

CA, for its part, said it believed the data had come from a good source, while the Trump campaign maintained that it had bought the users' details in good faith. The man who generated the data, CA researcher Alexsandr Kogan, told journalists he had broken no Facebook rules in harvesting the details of the 87 million friends and contacts of 270,000 entrants in the thisismydigitallife quiz he posted on the site in 2014. With everybody claiming innocence, the waters were muddied in 2018 when a former CA employee named Christopher Wylie and an ex-Facebook operations manager called Sandy Parakilas came forward with damaging allegations that CA knew the data was compromised and that Facebook had been aware for several years that its customers' information was not sufficiently protected. In the wave of recriminations that followed CA went out of business and Mark Zuckerberg embarked on a public apology tour where he vowed to put things right. This was not enough, however, to stave off a US$5 billion FTC fine for data privacy breaches, the largest-ever penalty of this type – but still, Facebook's critics complained, a drop in the ocean for such a wealthy corporation.

Whether Facebook knew more about CA's intentions and the Trump team's activities is still unclear. The same applies to any knowledge it may have had of Russian interference in the election (see pp.68–9), which was confirmed by the Mueller Report released in April 2018. But to get an idea of what Facebook stood to gain from a Trump victory in November 2016, it's worth looking back at the UK's Brexit referendum of June that year.

A FLAWED REFERENDUM?

In the summer of 2016, Facebook began displaying ads and posts allegedly originating from Russia aimed at influencing the Brexit referendum result in favour of Leave. For Russia, Brexit would significantly weaken the European Union, an institution Vladimir Putin regarded as a rival to his country's influence. Britain, especially London, was also a destination for stolen Russian state funds to be laundered through the capital's high-end property market. Detaching the UK from the EU, when it would no longer

Christopher Wylie, a former employee of Cambridge Analytica, alleged that Facebook was well aware that its customers' data was not being properly protected

be subject to strict tax and money laundering regulations, was phase one of the plan by Russia's leaders to make hiding their stolen assets easier; phase two was courting the British government so that it remained well-disposed to Russian investment in the capital, an aim achieved through generous campaign contributions to the ruling Conservative Party for the December 2019 general election (see p.69).

The extent of Russia's interference in the 2016 referendum was detailed in a report by Britain's intelligence services in October 2019. At the time of writing, this has yet to be published. Without access to this report the details of Russia's activities remain unknown, but one commonly held line of supposition runs that the main Brexit campaign group, Leave.EU, solicited help and cash from both Russia and Cambridge Analytica to achieve a Leave outcome. This took the form of mainly using Facebook (but also Twitter) to launch thousands of targeted ads and posts containing scare stories, fake news, false information and factual inaccuracies aimed at undermining support for Britain's continuing membership of the EU.

Whether you believe Facebook was a willing participant or not in an attempt to manipulate the thinking and voting intentions of millions of people, the Brexit referendum can plausibly be seen as a dress-rehearsal for the presidential election later that same year. This was a vote Facebook and the other big tech companies definitely had a stake in, with Donald Trump showing less inclination than Hillary Clinton to interfere with how the digital giants were regulated and how they arranged their tax and accounting affairs.

NATIONAL DIGITAL DEEP STATES

Not all digital deep states are corporate entities. In fact, because it is one of their duties to protect a country's security, national digital deep states can be far more direct in their attempts to gain a competitive advantage against their adversaries. The USA, Russia and North Korea have three of the most active cyber-security networks in operation today, so let's see how they go about their business.

Understanding America's NSA

As America's largest and most secretive intelligence service, the National Security Agency (NSA) was rocked when in 2013 one of its former contractors, Edward Snowden, went public with damaging revelations about its deep-state activities.

The details of every phone call going into and out of the US are kept by the NSA, Snowden revealed, authorized by post-9/11 legislation known as the Patriot Act and under a programme known as Ragtime-P. The NSA monitors all emails, texts, tweets, Facebook posts, credit card purchases and communications and transactions of every kind. It accesses the workings of the tech firms Yahoo, Facebook, AOL, Skype, Apple, Verizon, Microsoft, AT&T and Google, collecting two billion records a year in operations known as PRISM and MUSCULAR. With an army of hackers on its black books, it can infiltrate any computer or mobile device anywhere, roaming its files, installing spyware and malware, and taking control of its operations.

According to Snowden, the NSA has listening posts in all US embassies and consulates, and has, among many other infractions of international law, bugged the EU offices, listened in on German Chancellor Angela Merkel's phone calls and hacked the Brazilian president's emails. Much of this activity is done in partnership with NSA's British equivalent, GCHQ (Government Communications Headquarters).

In any country with a 'normal' judicial system many of the NSA's activities would be curtailed, but as well as having a secret secret service in the form of the NSA, America also has a secret legal system in the Foreign Intelligence Surveillance, or FISA, court. This body acts as a rubber stamp to the NSA's activities, giving them legitimacy they would otherwise lack. The court's decisions are almost never made public and we only know about its operations because Snowden included a FISA court authorization in his leaks. In 2013, the year of Snowden's revelations, the FISA court signed off on 1,800 surveillance orders and did not refuse a single NSA request.

As well as its defensive deep-state role, the NSA operates in an offensive capacity through US Cyber Command, or USCYBERCOM, which launches cyber-attacks on America's enemies, having declared the virtual world an 'operational domain', the online equivalent of a theatre of war. Its activities are super-secret, but in 2019 it was thought to have planted malware in Russia's national electrical grid, causing severe disruption. This was thought to be in retaliation for Russian hacks and cyber-attacks on American targets.

Inside Russia's troll farms

In April 2019, when special counsel Robert Mueller delivered his report into Russian interference in the 2016 US election, he indicted

12 of that country's intelligence officers for hacking offences. This confirmed what the world already knew: that Russia was a major hub of state-sponsored cyber-crime.

The officers were all employed by the Internet Research Agency (IRA) in St Petersburg, the world's most notorious 'troll farm'. Thought to be owned by Yevgeny Prighozin, a Russian oligarch with close ties to Vladimir Putin, the IRA exists to disrupt and destabilize foreign governments and businesses. IRA trolls use fake Facebook and Twitter accounts, blogposts and other social media to spread discord and disinformation on issues deemed harmful to Russia's interests. The IRA's pro-Donald Trump activities began in July 2015, one month after he declared his candidacy for president. A typical IRA Trumpian action was the June 2016 Facebook ad it purchased on behalf of the bogus United Muslims of America group advertising a 'Support Hillary, Save American Muslims' rally organized by IRA operatives in Washington D.C. in July 2016, just one of hundreds of illegal pro-Trump/anti-Hillary Clinton interventions. With the 2016 election won, the IRA was hard at work again in the 2018 US mid-terms on behalf of Republican candidates. In March 2020, with a US presidential election due in November, America's CNN news network reported that the IRA has established Trump re-election troll farms in Nigeria and Ghana, presumably in the hope that the NSA's all-seeing eye would not find them there.

Russia's military secret service, the GRU, also engages in cyber-attacks against rival nations. It backed both the Sandworm cyber-attack on Ukraine's power grid in 2015 and the Fancy Bear hack on the US Democratic National Committee's (DNC) servers in the run-up to the 2016 US election, filtering the stolen emails through Wikileaks, the website that has been described both as a tireless campaigner against establishment lies and corruption and a stooge or 'useful idiot' for the Kremlin's deep state. In June 2017, GRU hackers launched what has been described as the most devastating cyber-attack in history. NotPetya was malware originally targeted at Ukraine but it spread worldwide rapidly and indiscriminately, paralysing the international shipping company Maersk, the European courier TNT Express and the pharmaceutical manufacturer Merck among hundreds of other organizations at an estimated cost of US$10 billion. It even hit the Russian state oil company, Rosneft. Ironically, NotPetya was enabled by a penetration tool called EternalBlue, which Russian hackers stole from the NSA.

North Korea's Department of Digital Crime

Known as Office 39, North Korea's feared digital-security agency is a highly skilled army of 6,000 hackers whose main activities are launching destabilizing cyber-attacks on South Korea and America and the cyber-theft of funds from banks, companies and financial institutions worldwide.

Once trained, many Office 39 operatives are sent abroad to pose as overseas workers or students. It's thought that around 20 per cent of North Korea's hackers are based in India, with significant numbers in Malaysia, Vietnam, Kenya, Mozambique and New Zealand. For many years a hub of Office 39 digital crime was located in the basement of the Chilbosan Hotel in China's Liaoning province, just across North Korea's border. In 2018 the Chinese government was forced to close the hotel to avoid international sanctions and the hackers moved on. One reason North Korean hackers work abroad is because the country's own internet service is both poorly run and tightly controlled. Known as Kwangmyong, it operates more like a corporate intranet system, with very limited access to anything beyond its highly secure firewalls.

Regardless of where North Korea's hackers are located, their targets are predictably easy to locate. Analysts estimate that every day, around 1.5 million attacks are launched against South Korea by its northern neighbour's computers. The first hacking assaults began in 2009, against government departments, banks and corporations. In 2011 the 'Ten Days of Rain' malware severely disrupted South

Korea's Nonghyup Bank and this was followed in 2013 by a larger 'DarkSeoul' attack on South Korea's three largest banks and media companies, stealing and erasing sensitive customer and corporate data at an estimated cost of US$800 million.

The next year, North Korean hackers were blamed for infiltrating Sony Pictures' systems and holding the company to ransom until it pulled the release of *The Interview*, a comedy about a bungled plot to assassinate North Korea's leader, Kim Jong-un. This represented a move into international hacking, exemplified in the 'Wannacry' ransomware attack in 2017, where 230,000 computer systems worldwide, including those of the NHS in the UK, were infected with a virus that threatened to erase data unless each of the hundreds of thousands of users affected paid US$300 in bitcoin. Fortunately, the hackers miscoded their program, meaning they were unable to collect any payments. Nevertheless, the attack caused billions of dollars of damage.

By 2018 an elite group of North Korean hackers had launched the wide-ranging 'Reaper' and 'GhostSecret' attacks on international banks, financial markets, healthcare systems and corporations. One of their early successes was the theft in January 2018 of US$440 million from the Tokyo-based digital money exchange operator Coincheck, which forced the company out of business. It remains one of the largest cryptocurrency robberies ever. Agencies such as the NSA and Cyber Command in America are of course fighting back, and the two countries are engaged in a virtual war that will only escalate as digital technology becomes increasingly sophisticated.

The development of digital deep states is proof of the endless ambition and ingenuity of vested interests to win at all costs. All deep states – digital and three-dimensional – thrive best in the shadows. Exposing their activities to light is the first step towards curbing or even ending their activities and showing their co-conspirators in government and other positions of power that they no longer have the free hand they have always enjoyed. How the secret power networks will react to ever-closer scrutiny and public exposure will be interesting, to say the least. One definite trend appears to be the deliberate destabilizing not just of our institutions but of our systems of belief, too, and the deep states' creation of a post-truth world of alternative facts, parallel realities and true lies has been one of its most effective achievements of recent years. In a world where no one believes anything any more, the lies of the deep states can more easily pass unseen.

INDEX

PICTURE CREDITS